BLUE · GRAY · BLACK

MY SERVICE TO COUNTRY

BLUE · GRAY · BLACK
MY SERVICE TO COUNTRY

By

Don Cesare

East of the Mountains and West of the Sun

RHYOLITE PRESS, LLC
Colorado Springs, Colorado

Published in the United States of America by Rhyolite Press, LLC
P.O. Box 2406
Colorado Springs, Colorado 80901
www.rhyolitepress.com

Cesare, Donald J.
Blue·Gray·Black   My Service to Country
1st edition   November, 2015

Library of Congress Control Number: 2015954410

ISBN 978-1-943829-02-6

eBook ISBN 978-1-943829-03-3

PRINTED IN THE UNITED STATES OF AMERICA

10 9 8 7 6 5 4 3 2 1

Book design by Dave Rickert
Cover design by Donald Kallaus
Author photo, © Dave Rickert, 2015

For
my wife Jan and daughter Ann,
without whose support and encouragement
this book might not have been completed.

CONTENTS

CHAPTERS

FOREWORD

Most of us consider ourselves fortunate to witness something of historical importance in our lifetimes. Few of us have the opportunity to be a participant in such events. Don Cesare was directly involved in several—the operations of the highly secret U-2 spy plane, the training of the Tibetan guerilla resistance fighters, and the investigations of both the assassination of President John Kennedy and of the murders of three civil rights workers in Mississippi by the Ku Klux Klan. That's extraordinary. But what has made Don's life especially unusual, perhaps unique, is that he has played a role in history serving in three of the country's most prestigious organizations—as an officer in the United States Marine Corps, as an agent of the Central Intelligence Agency, and for more than 20 years as a special agent with the Federal Bureau of Investigation, part of his service taking place when I was privileged to be the FBI's director. Don's exciting career, spanning nearly four decades, has reflected his selfless and constant dedication to the nation.

William H. Webster
FBI Director, 1978 - 1987
CIA Director, 1987 - 1991

PREFACE

My father was the chief of police in a small Pennsylvania town. His example inspired me to pursue a career in law enforcement. In that field, my goal was to become a special agent with the Federal Bureau of Investigation (FBI). I achieved that objective but not before my life went down some other interesting paths. This book is about those experiences as well as my career in the FBI. I have been fortunate along the way to have been not only an eyewitness to but also a participant in some of the significant events of the twentieth century.

After graduating from Bloomsburg State College in Pennsylvania, I enlisted in the U. S. Marine Corps Reserve and attended Officer Candidates School at Marine Corps Base, Quantico, Virginia. Ironically, my class was billeted next to the FBI Academy which was located on the base, and I was able to observe some of the Bureau's training firsthand. While on active duty as an officer in the Marine Corps, I was assigned to the Sixth Fleet in the Mediterranean where I had my first experience in law enforcement—as a shore patrol officer in the fleet's ports of call. My years in the Corps also brought discipline and maturity and a strong desire to continue to serve my country in whatever I did the rest of my life.

Shortly after completing active service with the Marine Corps and encouraged by another Marine officer, I applied to the Central Intelligence Agency (CIA). Visions of adventure and intrigue filled my mind. In the CIA, I served initially in Turkey as a security officer for the Agency's high altitude aircraft reconnaissance program, the U-2. After that assignment, I was transferred to the CIA's Far East Division as a paramilitary officer. In that role, my job was to train Tibetans to fight the Communist Chinese who had invaded their homeland. The training took place in the mountains of Colorado and on the island of Saipan in the western Pacific. My work for the CIA was interesting and I learned much, but my eye was always on a career in the FBI.

Early in 1963, I resigned from the CIA, applied to the FBI, and was appointed a special agent. I had finally reached my goal. My career with the Bureau which spanned more than twenty years included participation in the investigations of the assassination of President John F. Kennedy and the murder of three civil rights workers in Mississippi by the Ku Klux Klan. In the latter case—made famous in the movie *Mississippi Burning*—I handled the Bureau's chief informant. The evidence he supplied destroyed the Klan's empire in Mississippi.

Although I occasionally drew on other sources, this book relies largely on my own recollections of the events it describes. I alone am responsible for any errors of fact or interpretation that it may contain.

CHAPTER 1

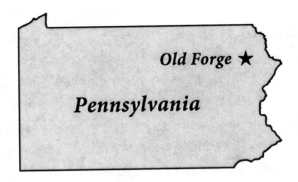

Old Forge ★

Pennsylvania

EARLY YEARS

Old Forge, the town where I was born on July 20, 1930, is a small borough located in the northeast section of Pennsylvania, just a few miles south of Scranton. It acquired its name in a contest. My father, Primo Cesare, who had been chief of police, loved to tell a story about how the borough got its name. His version said there were two forges, both located along the Lackawanna River (which runs the entire length of the borough) and close to each other. One was constructed in the late 1700s and was known as the old forge; the other, built several years after the first, was called, not very imaginatively, the new forge. To name the borough, the citizens devised a contest—whichever of the two forges could shoe a horse the fastest would be able to name the place. (I can only assume that these folks were a betting bunch.) The old forge won!

The town is very ordinary and has changed over the centuries from a mining community to a typical Eastern suburb. It had always boasted an excellent public school system. In 1935, President

Franklin Roosevelt signed the Social Security Act, and the country was emerging from the Depression. That year was also notable because, at the age of five, I entered Old Forge's public schools. Why had I started so early? (It was something I regretted later on because I was always a little behind my peers in school when it came to maturity.) It seems I put up a big fuss when my boyhood friend, Joe Taffera, who was a year older than I, was being taken to school by his oldest sister, Ursula. My antics resulted in my mother, Edna, yelling to Ursula, "Go ahead and take him too." As a result, I graduated high school at age sixteen, a year younger than my classmates.

My father was known to his many friends as "Chief," and carried this title to his dying day. To me he was "Pop," and I was proud that he was my father. During my early school years I was always referred to as "the chief's son" and, consequently, given a wide berth in schoolyard activities. Some of my earliest boyhood memories were of my Pop in his police uniform which fascinated me. He was a large man, resplendent in his grey, steel-colored tunic with his shiny Sam Browne belt, a gold badge, and, of course, the leather leggings. This indelible image of my father cultivated in me a lifelong interest in law enforcement. In our discussions, he stressed that if I were to

Official photograph of my father, Primo A. Cesare, chief of police, Old Forge, Pennsylvania (Author's personal collection).

choose such a career, it should be in the FBI. It was, in his view, the most professional of all law enforcement organizations.

Pop was a strict disciplinarian and, on one occasion when I was very young, gave me a warning I never forgot. He said with a deep voice and clenched teeth that if I ever brought disgrace to our family name he would come down on me hard. I was the first born of three children and so was the pathfinder for my brother, Carl, and my sister, Marie. Although I experienced the joys of early boyhood in a small town, I never forgot my father's threat. His admonishment always came to mind whenever I was confronted with a boyhood crisis or, for that matter, crises later in life.

My primary and secondary education in the Old Forge public schools was very good, primarily because of caring and capable teachers. I combined good scholarship with some athletic ability and, upon graduation from high school in 1947, was awarded an athletic scholarship to the University of Scranton. Elio Ghigiarelli, a distant relative, Scranton alumnus, and one of the school's legendary athletes recommended me for the scholarship. He was a successful and well-known football and basketball coach in the area, and, although I never played for him, he always supported my athletic endeavors. Unfortunately, I spent only a short time at the University of Scranton. I was too immature to appreciate the opportunity I had. My studies were not a problem, but on the football field the freshmen were practice dummies for the varsity. We were matched against returning veterans who were older than we were, often ten years older. This mismatch beat me down. After the football season ended, I left the university in part because of the pounding I took on the football field but also because I was living at home and had a very long bus commute to the campus every day. All of this discouraged me. Nonetheless, I resolved to return to college at some point.

After staying out of school for a semester I enrolled at Bloomsburg State College (now Bloomsburg University), which is located in the eastern Pennsylvania town for which it is named. At Bloomsburg, I enjoyed campus life, played football for three seasons, and felt that I had matured. I held a part-time job assisting the janitorial staff (mostly with a broom), and was paid $21 a month, the college's equivalent of an athletic scholarship. My experience at Bloomsburg was completely different from that at the University of Scranton. At Bloomsburg, I lived away from home, was part of the college community, and came under the influence of a man who had a profound effect on my life—John Hoch. He was the dean of men at the college and always found time to counsel me. I did well academically and graduated with honors in 1952. I was especially proud to deliver the Ivy Day Oration during commencement activities. Unfortunately, the Ivy Day ritual, a tradition for over fifty years, has fallen out of fashion at Bloomsburg. It featured a ceremony with music, a speech, and the planting of ivy. At the conclusion of my speech we planted

Edna, my mother, a driving force in my life. (Author's personal collection)

ivy at Old Waller Hall, creating "ivy-covered halls." My father commented that I looked like a priest sermonizing in my black robe. My mother, who always urged me on, said, "Now make something of yourself." And indeed I did—I joined the U. S. Marine Corps.

In fact, I joined the Marines in May 1952 immediately following my college graduation ceremony. As soon as I took off my cap and gown, I anxiously hitchhiked to the Marine Corps recruiting office in Wilkes-Barre, Pennsylvania, and was sworn into the Marine Corps Reserve. I then returned to Bloomsburg and worked as the town's water safety director until I was called to active duty on September 30, 1952.

CHAPTER 2

GLOBE AND ANCHOR DAYS

My orders directed me to report to Marine Corps Base Quantico, Virginia, to attend Officer Candidates School (OCS). The course was a humbling experience: we were all treated the same—like dogs, but college dogs! The curriculum was primarily physical with a minimum of classroom work. The first indication we were in for it occurred shortly after we arrived. The noncoms (noncommissioned officers) who were the drill instructors (DIs) lined us up in formation. One of the DIs asked each candidate what he wanted to be in the Marine Corps. Some wanted to be air wing pilots, so they had to spread their arms and "fly" around the parade ground. Others wanted to be tankers, so they were told to get down on all fours and make and sound like a tank. The artillery wannabes were boom-booming all over the place. It was a humiliating sight, and much enjoyed by our oppressors, the DIs. Running the obstacle course was a daily routine, and the instructors never failed to make it more challenging by coating the over-the-water obstacles with mud to ensure that you went into the drink. We also played a lot of "King of the Hill." This contest pitted one platoon against another. The objective was for one platoon to push a large ball up toward a position at the top of the hill that was defended by another platoon. It was mayhem but fun.

I graduated from OCS number one in my platoon. I think I was able to deceive my DI into thinking I was a gung ho Marine. In reality, I just wanted to put the miserable experience behind me! At our graduation exercises, I was commissioned a second lieutenant in the Marine Corps Reserve—the youngest in my class.

Upon graduating from Officer Candidates School, I received an allowance to buy uniform items prior to entering the next training course, the Marine Corps Basic School, also at Quantico. These purchases included a set of the Corps' splendid dress blues. We were also granted several days leave before the Basic School course started after the Christmas holidays. I used this time to go home to Old Forge, where I was anxious to wear my dress blues to impress a young lady I had been writing to while I was at OCS. I looked forward to the date and confidently expected to wow her in my uniform. I meticulously put on the dress blues in my old bedroom at home and descended the stairs, anxious to show my mom and dad how I looked. As I entered the kitchen, my mother, who was never at a loss for words, said, "My God, you look like a lion tamer!" My ego was deflated—I returned to the bedroom and put on a much less glamorous brown corduroy suit to wear on the date.

In Basic School we learned the role of a Marine infantry lieutenant in modern warfare. We were losing so many lieutenants in Korea that the school changed the name of the course from the platoon "leaders' " to the platoon "commanders' " course. They evidently felt that redefining the lieutenant's role—from always leading out front to commanding but not always leading out front—would reduce the losses.

Although Basic School training was deadly serious, it was not without its humorous incidents. A newly commissioned second lieutenant, celebrating his new status, was involved in a knock-down-drag-out party in the Wardman Park Hotel on Connecticut Avenue in Washington, D.C. During the festivities the new lieutenant, on a dare, took off his uniform, leaving him completely naked, and climbed down outside from the third floor to the main floor. He then tried to climb back, but, unfortunately, entered a second-floor apartment, rather than the third-floor apartment from which he had started. Sadly for the lieutenant, the apartment belonged to a retired admiral whose wife, very familiar with naval attire, immediately determined that this young man was out of uniform, and contacted the authorities. The last I heard, the formerly naked lieutenant was fully clothed and waiting to see the commandant of the Marine Corps.

My first assignment following graduation from Basic School was to the Fleet Marine Force at Camp Lejeune, North Carolina, and to the fabled 6th Marine Regiment as a platoon commander. We were constantly in the field, both day and night, on maneuvers simulating beach landings, practicing vertical envelopments, and solving problems dealing with fortified positions. Our commander repeatedly assured us that we would all wind up in Korea. My battalion, however (and to the surprise of almost all of us), was selected to provide the landing force for the U. S. Sixth Fleet, which was stationed in the Mediterranean.

Attack transport USS Sarasota (APA 204) in Mediterranean, 1954 (Courtesy, U.S. Navy)

On May 5, 1954 my unit, the 1st Battalion, 6th Marines (Reinforced), consisting of 1,700 officers and enlisted men, boarded the ships of Transport Division 25 and began a five-month, 25,000-mile journey and tour of duty with the Sixth Fleet. After visiting numerous ports in several countries throughout the Mediterranean, the cruise culminated in a North Atlantic Treaty Organization (NATO) exercise with troops from allied nations. Known as Operation Keystone, it was so successful that we received a "well done" from the task force commander.

I would be remiss if I did not emphasize the profound effects this cruise had on my unit, and on me personally. After participating in four amphibious operations throughout the Mediterranean, we developed a great sense of unit identity and a high degree of esprit de corps. Operating with military forces from other nations, including British Royal Marines, French Foreign Legionnaires, and Greek, Italian, and Turkish troops, matured our battalion landing team (as the unit was commonly referred to). Toward the end of our cruise a rumor circulated that we were going through the Suez Canal en route to Southeast Asia to assist French forces that were overrun by the communists in French Indochina. Although we didn't go, our excitement was genuine. I have always regretted that our unit was never tested in combat; I am confident we would have done well.

Author onboard USS Sarasota, 1954 (Author's personal collection)

The cruise also affected me personally. I visited three continents and seven foreign countries, and participated in demanding military operations with troops from other nations. These experiences matured me, developed my leadership ability, and strengthened my appreciation for my own country. Before each of our amphibious landings we received an intelligence briefing on the country we were entering. These briefings covered the country's geography, topography, population, social customs, and natural resources. They gave me an appreciation for intelligence and aroused my interest in that field.

During our stay in Naples, Italy, I went to Rome, primarily to see some of the historical sites that had been described in my Latin classes in high school. I was enthralled to stand in the ruins of the Colosseum and to see the Pantheon, the Roman Forum, and the city's basilicas, in particular St. Peter's Basilica. While at St. Peter's I found myself on the outer edges of a crowd of 60,000 packed into the huge edifice for the solemn mass canonizing (declaring) the former pope, Pius X, to be a saint. After the mass, the current pope, Pius XII, was borne aloft in the papal chair and carried from the church. He then reappeared on the papal balcony and blessed the crowd, estimated at 350,000, that had gathered in St. Peter's Square below. I was among them; it was a momentous event in my life. As a devout Catholic, I realized that I had witnessed the historic canonization of a pope of the Roman Catholic Church.

After the cruise, and while stationed at Camp Lejeune, I came in contact with Major Wysoski, an old China hand, who had served with the Office of Strategic Services (the legendary OSS) in World War II. He was in charge of field training for reserve units. I worked for him and we developed a good relationship. When he heard I was thinking about returning to civilian life, he told me to consider working for the organization that had replaced the OSS, the Central Intelligence Agency (the CIA, or simply, the "Agency"). I told him I was interested, and he said he would arrange for an interview. In about two weeks I received a letter asking me to go to Washington, D.C., on a certain date and check into the Roger Smith Hotel. At the hotel, two individuals interviewed me, administered a polygraph exam, and gave me a variety of personality tests. I recall some of the interview questions. One was whether accepting a position with the CIA would interfere with my Marine Corps Reserve status? (I said that it would not and added that a Marine officer would be an asset to any organization.) Another was whether I had any plans to be married in the next few years? (I said that I did not.) Last, was I averse to lengthy periods of assignment overseas? (Again, I answered no.) At the conclusion of the interview, we parted on what I thought were positive terms. I then requested release from active duty in the Marine Corps and waited to hear from the Agency. With no word after what I thought was an inordinate amount of time, I began to think that maybe my polygraph test results had disqualified me, for I had admitted to keeping my nice soft (after many washings) Marine Corps blanket. This was in response to the question, "Did you ever take anything from the government?" Finally a letter arrived, and I was instructed to report to the Agency as a security officer.

CHAPTER 3

WITH THE CIA: SECURITY OFFICER FOR THE U-2

In June 1957, I reported to I Building at CIA headquarters, then in the District of Columbia. This building, like its immediate neighbors J, K, and L Buildings, housed the Agency's various operational and administrative components. These "temporary," run-down structures, built in 1923, could not have been sitting on more hallowed ground. They were close to the city's historic landmarks, including the Washington Monument, the Lincoln and Jefferson Memorials, and the White House. I visited these and other famous places frequently, usually during my lunch hour.

Upon reporting to the security office in I Building, I was directed to the "Rock Desk" where I found out that I, along with others, had been hired to provide security for the "Rock Project." Although the briefing we received was very sketchy, I learned that this operation involved high-altitude aircraft reconnaissance flights over the Soviet Union. In my conversations with the other new employees, I discovered that all of us had served in the military; were college graduates; were able to go anywhere, anytime; and planned to remain single for at least two years. Much later, I learned that these were the prime requisites for entry into the Rock Group, the unit of security agents assigned to the project.

We were granted provisional security clearances, photographed for the Agency and for passports, and received numerous inoculations required for overseas assignment. We were then told to report to the Matomic Building located in downtown Washington, the center of the security operations for the Rock Project.

At the Matomic Building, we received a detailed briefing on the project. We were told that the Agency was overflying the Soviet heartland to collect intelligence using a revolutionary jet-powered aircraft known as the U-2. I learned that it had been developed by the Lockheed Aircraft Corporation in just 90 days in 1955. However, I later found out that Kelly Johnson, the aircraft's designer, had been working on a design for what became the U-2 since early 1954. In early 1955, the CIA gave Lockheed a contract to produce a prototype, which was delivered ahead of schedule on July 25, 1955. The U-2 was able to fly for long distances at 70,000 feet. It was equipped with exceptionally high-resolution cameras that could photograph objects on the ground from high altitude with the utmost clarity. The images were so sharp they appeared to have been taken from two or three feet away.

The U-2 operated from three sites under the cover of the National Advisory Committee for Aeronautics (NACA) ostensibly to study weather phenomena in various parts of the world. (In 1958, NACA became the National Aeronautics and Space Administration, NASA.) One unit, known as Weather Reconnaissance Squadron (Provisional) had been sent originally to Lakenheath, England, but was relocated to Giebelstadt, West Germany, about the time I started working for the Agency. U-2s in another unit, known as Weather Reconnaissance Squadron Provisional III, flew out of Atsugi Naval Air Station in Japan. The unit to which I was assigned as a security officer, the Second Weather Operational Squadron (Provisional)—informally known as Detachment 10-10—was stationed at Adana Air Base (renamed Incirlik Air Base in 1958 after a town near the large city of Adana) in southeastern Turkey, not far from the Mediterranean and the Syrian border.

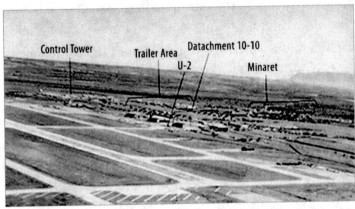

Incirlik Air Base, Adana, Turkey, ca. 1957, from which U-2s of Detachment 10-10 made overflights of the Soviet Union. (Courtesy, Department of Defense)

After I received my official orders, I picked up a passport which indicated I was a Department of Air Force civilian employee, and in late July 1957 flew on a military transport to Incirlik, where I joined the team that provided round-the-clock security for the U-2. At Incirlik I saw this remarkable bird for the first time. It was painted a very dark blue (almost black, but with no markings) to match the surrounding sky at cruising altitude. It had a slender, 63-foot long fuselage and narrow wings, spanning 103 feet. On each side of the fuselage were intakes which fed air into the single, J57 turbojet engine. The cockpit looked to me to be extremely cramped, apparently the reason so many of the U-2 pilots were all small in stature. Underneath the fuselage was the landing gear, in a bicycle configuration (rather than the tricycle landing gear found on most aircraft), and what we called "pogo sticks." These were actually two, hard-rubber wheels attached to steel "legs" that fit into slots under each wing, provided stability during taxi and takeoff, and were designed to drop off as the U-2 left the ground. One of our duties was to retrieve the pogo sticks after the aircraft lifted off. Then, during landing, when the U-2's wingtips dropped down and made contact with the runway, we would rush forward, right the wings, and insert the pogo sticks. The first time I assisted in a recovery I made the mistake of grabbing the wingtip and burned my hand. It was a hard-learned lesson; afterward I carried gloves and avoided the wingtips whenever possible. Once the pogo sticks were in place, we escorted the aircraft as the pilot taxied it to its hangar in our secure compound.

U-2 aircraft with "pogo sticks" under wings.
(Courtesy, National Museum of the U.S. Air Force)

U-2 overflight and border surveillance missions provided the CIA and the Air Force with invaluable intelligence on Soviet nuclear testing and missile launches. After an aircraft returned from its mission, technicians removed the equipment containing the photography and other data that had been gathered and delivered it to intelligence specialists in our compound. After they made a quick assessment, the material was placed in secure canisters and handcarried to CIA headquarters by an armed member of our security unit. Sometimes we were assigned to dispose of used film by burning it in a pit located in a remote area of the base. I vividly recall a conversation I had with Ed Wilson, another security team member, on one of these burn missions. We notified the tower of the intended burn and dumped the film into the pit after dousing it with gasoline. We constantly stoked the fire to ensure all the film was destroyed. While we were burning the film, Ed and I shot the bull and shared a laugh. He asked me why I had joined the Agency. I told him I wanted adventure and the opportunity to serve my country. I then asked him the same question. He replied without hesitation that he wanted to make money. I asked him how the hell he thought he was going to make money working for the government. Years later, I found out how Ed fulfilled his goal. After leaving the Agency in 1971, he made millions in the illegal arms trade, and was able to buy estates around the world and live opulently. His clandestine international arms trafficking earned him the name "Death Merchant." But he was eventually caught, convicted of selling arms and explosives to Libya, and served twenty-two years in prison for his treasonous acts.

The heroes of the U-2 operation were the pilots, the "drivers," as we called them. All were Air Force officers, paid by the Agency and "sheep-dipped" (disguised as civilians working for Lockheed under contract to NACA to hide their military status). All were excellent pilots, thoroughly familiar with the U-2's special equipment, including its sophisticated cameras, and with their designated targets and routes they would fly to them.

U-2 designer Kelly Johnson (left) with pilot Francis Gary Powers. (Courtesy, National Museum of the U. S. Air Force)

During my assignment at Incirlik, several events caused the U-2 detachment to be especially active: the Suez Crisis of 1956, test flights of Soviet ICBMs (intercontinental ballistic missiles) in August and September 1957, and the successful launches of the Sputnik earth-orbiting satellites in October and November 1957. Fortunately, we had additional U-2 assets available (the existence of the detachment in Germany had been compromised and moved to Incirlik). The increase in U-2 missions meant that we, as security agents, traveled frequently from Turkey to Washington, D.C., with canisters of film for interpretation by the Agency.

The heightened activity, of course, affected the "drivers" the most; they were getting as much flight time as they wanted or could handle. Among them, Francis Gary (Frank) Powers was, no doubt, the busiest. He was an outstanding aviator who, at the time, had the most operational time in the U-2. He was not only an extraordinary flyer but also a friendly and affable man who always had time for others. These qualities made him a popular figure in the detachment. Powers had flown the first overflight of Soviet territory from Incirlik in November of 1956, a mission that required thorough and intense planning and presidential approval. On May 1, 1960, Powers' U-2, on a mission originating from a base in Pakistan, was hit by a Soviet surface-to-air missile. Powers parachuted to safety, but was captured, put on trial for espionage, and sentenced to seven years' hard labor. In February 1962, after 21 months in prison, he was freed, in exchange for the release of a Soviet spy. Buster Edens was another outstanding "driver" who was also popular in the Incirlik detachment. He was built like a football player; I was amazed that a person of his size could squeeze into that U-2 cockpit. He was killed in a U-2 accident at Edwards Air Force Base, California, in 1965. Al Rand, also a U-2 pilot, became a favorite of mine after he took me up in the detachment's T-33 jet. He literally wrung me out during the flight.

In addition to the pilots, the Incirlik detachment was made up of other Air Force personnel, Agency types, and contractors. All were talented and energetic. Morale was high, with everyone focused on the mission, which we recognized as vital to our country. We lived in trailers designated for the three different groups. Although we worked well together, we pretty much socialized within our own group. The area around Adana was full of historic sites—Crusader castles, Roman aqueducts and baths, and ancient tombs. My coworkers and I spent much of our free time exploring these ruins. Also, the beaches in the southeast part of Turkey along the Mediterranean were beautiful and unspoiled. We used them whenever we could find time. In part because of these attractions, I very much enjoyed my tour of duty at Incirlik.

In early 1957, a new U-2 unit, designated Detachment C, Weather Reconnaissance Squadron Provisional III, opened at the Atsugi Naval Air Station located fifteen miles west of Yokohama, Japan. I was transferred there in late 1959. During my tour, the detachment overflew Communist China frequently. Also, it deployed to Cubi Point in the Philippines, both launching and recovering aircraft at that location. While at Atsugi, I found a different attitude from that at Incirlik. In Japan, it seemed to me that there was little interplay among Agency, Air Force, and contractor personnel. The job got done, but without the camaraderie I was used to at Incirlik. Although I don't think it affected detachment morale, the crash landing of a U-2 at a small airfield near Tokyo created some unpleasant publicity. The Japanese media covered the crash extensively and published pictures of the aircraft. The incident was magnified when security guards from Atsugi arrived at the scene and ordered the curious crowd away at gunpoint.

During my tour in Japan, I made several trips from Atsugi to the U. S. mainland, usually delivering the film canisters to an Agency representative at Travis Air Force Base in northern California. I assumed they were headed to the Agency's Photographic Intelligence Center, located at that time in Washington, D.C.

Our group provided continuous security to the U-2 operations at Atsugi and in the Philippines. We often talked (among ourselves, of course) that the only ones who did not know the true nature of the U-2 program were the American people. Certainly the Soviets knew much about the U-2 from radar tracking and other intelligence means, as likely did the Chinese who used Soviet radars in their own air defense system. In one of their aviation publications, the Soviets had described the U-2 as a strategic reconnaissance aircraft, but, strangely, after initially protesting the flights in 1956, did not object to them again. Our security group felt that because the Soviets were having such success with Sputnik and their ICBM program, admitting that Soviet MiG fighters could not reach the U-2's cruising altitude would have detracted from those achievements. While still assigned to the U-2 program, I heard that Premier Nikita Khrushchev, when congratulated on the success of the Soviet missile program at a Washington function during his visit to the United States in 1959, replied: "Yes, but you Americans have the cameras."

As my time in the U-2 program drew to a close, I reflected that I had likely been participating in a venture of historic importance. Many contributed to the program's success: Kelly Johnson, the brilliant aeronautical engineer from Lockheed, who designed the U-2; Richard Bissell, then chief of the Agency's clandestine services and the U-2 program's driving force, whom I met during one of his visits to our detachment at Incirlik; the courageous and skilled pilots who flew the aircraft (with Frank Powers leading the list); and, finally, all the Agency, Air Force, and contractor personnel who worked together to accomplish the U-2's mission. Even the Soviets recognized the U-2 as the single greatest breakthrough in the history of intelligence collection.

After approximately a year in the Far East, I was sent back to Washington, D.C., to attend the Agency's security agent training course. It was held in another set of "temporary" buildings that had been constructed to house the OSS during World War II and that the Agency would continue to use until the early 1960s when it moved to Langley, Virginia. The course material included the role and responsibilities of the CIA director in the intelligence community, the missions of the various groups within the Agency, firearms training, and extensive instruction on locks and safes. We also had to undergo a polygraph examination, apparently standard procedure for Agency personnel who were coming off a project—any project. Upon completing the course, we were recognized as security agents and assigned to field offices located throughout the United States. I didn't go far. My orders were to report to the Agency's headquarters field office, also in D.C., which handled only "special assignments."

I soon found that "special assignments" amounted to providing security for defectors—in essence, the security agents were their baby-sitters. Once defectors arrived in the United States, they were usually put up in safe houses that were located in the D.C. suburbs and maintained by the Agency. Our job was to provide continuous protection for the defector and his family (if he had any), not only at the safe house, but wherever they might go. I received this boring assignment often, usually protecting Polish government officials and military officers. One of my last assignments of this kind involved the defection of a young Soviet naval officer who was accompanied by his Polish sweetheart. They were known to me and my colleagues as "Nick and Eva." After their arrival in the United States, they were located in a safe house in northern Virginia. Two other security agents and I were assigned to protect them. During the day, the couple underwent intense debriefings, not only by Agency personnel but also by agents from the Office of Naval Intelligence. We learned that "Nick" was, in reality, Capt. Nikolai Federovich Artamonov, who at twenty-seven had been the youngest commanding officer of a destroyer in Soviet naval history. While on a tour of duty in Poland, Artamonov met a medical student, Eva Gora. They fell in love, sought asylum in Sweden in 1959, and were brought to the United States by the CIA. Artamonov was given a new identity, Nicholas George Shadrin, and employed, first, as an analyst with Office of Naval Intelligence, and then as a translator for the Defense Intelligence Agency. Shadrin was tall (about six feet two), very assertive, and with a serious demeanor. He appeared to me to be overly concerned with his girlfriend, Eva, who would later become his wife. I was assigned to protect the couple for about ten days soon after their arrival, but did not know their background. Years later when the Shadrin story became known I made the connection. Shadrin enjoyed close relationships with the U. S. military and intelligence communities in the Washington area. The Soviets convicted Captain Artamonov (Shadrin's former identity) of treason and sentenced him to death in absentia. After being contacted in 1966 by the KGB, the Soviet secret police, Shadrin agreed to work as a U.S. intelligence agent. During an assignment to Vienna in 1975 he disappeared, apparently kidnapped and possibly murdered by the KGB.

CHAPTER 4

WITH THE CIA:
TRAINING TIBETAN FREEDOM FIGHTERS

In time, I became dissatisfied with my position as a security agent, and decided to take the drastic step of "shopping my file." In Agency terms this meant that I was looking for a new position at the CIA, had rejected the security agent career specialty, and would never be able to return to it. It was a desperate move, but I was determined to find a more adventurous job within the Agency. After undergoing an exit interview with the Office of Security, I began walking the hallways of the Agency's temporary buildings in Washington, searching for an office that could use a former Marine Corps captain and security agent with several years of experience overseas. When I visited the Far East Division (headed by the powerful and respected Desmond Fitzgerald), I was instructed to contact its Tibetan desk. Here I met Roger McCarthy, who was in charge of the Agency's Tibetan project. I was immediately drawn to Roger, and considered him a "man's man." I assume he also liked what he saw in me because he offered me a job.

McCarthy, who had headed the Agency's Tibetan project since early 1959, explained to me that when Communist China's People's Liberation Army (PLA) invaded Tibet in 1950, the Tibetans resisted at first, but were no match for the PLA because they were ill-prepared, disorganized, badly outnumbered, and lacked modern military skills, weapons, and other equipment. In 1956, the Tibetans, who realized that the price of incorporation into China had been forfeiture of their religious freedom and national independence, began armed resistance against the Chinese occupiers. In March 1959, the Tibetans staged an uprising in Lhasa, the country's capital. The resulting Communist Chinese crackdown was brutal with tens of thousands killed. (In the twenty years between the beginning of the Tibetan armed resistance in 1956 and end of the Cultural Revolution in China in 1976, estimates are that 1,200,000 Tibetans lost their lives and more than 6,000 religious sites in the country were destroyed.) Ironically, the Dalai Lama, the country's religious leader who was opposed to all forms of violence, fled to India during the uprising in Lhasa and formed a government in exile. (Although McCarthy never admitted it to me, some of my associates indicated that he had played a key role in the Dalai Lama's escape.) The example of fierce resistance by the Tibetans encouraged the United States to provide support to the rebels in the form of

Roger McCarthy, CIA, head of the Tibetan project and my mentor. (Author's personal collection)

covert assistance by the CIA.

Prior to my assignment in the field as part of these operations, McCarthy asked me to accompany him to the Armed Forces Staff College in Norfolk, Virginia, to hear several presentations by French Army Col. David Galula, the author of several books on counterinsurgency warfare. He was one of the most influential and celebrated counterinsurgency experts of his time and a leading authority on Mao Tse-tung's revolutionary warfare tactics. McCarthy felt that we might be able to pick up some valuable information that would aid our Tibetan resistance fighters.

Galula's presentations dealt with his experiences in China and Algeria. In China, he had observed that Mao's guerrilla tactics emphasized winning the allegiance and support of the population and demonstrated how an inferior military force could succeed against one that was larger and better equipped. We were both heartened and cautioned by these observations. As McCarthy explained, the Tibetan resistance fighters surely would have the support of their people, but the situation was different than in China. McCarthy said the Tibetans that he trained initially at the CIA station on the island of Saipan in the western Pacific were mostly members of the Dalai Lama's palace guard—competent, loyal, and fierce fighters, but who, no matter how much "hit and run" guerrilla warfare was stressed, would often choose to stay in contact with enemy forces and fight it out. We would have to make a special effort in our training program to convince the Tibetans of the value of "hit-and-run" tactics in harassing and disrupting the PLA.

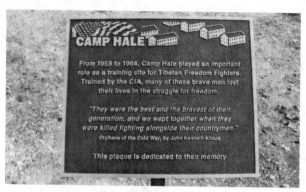

Commemorative plaque dedicated to the Tibetan
Freedom Fighters, Camp Hale, Colorado.
(Author's personal collection)

I arrived at Camp Hale, the CIA's training site for the Tibetans in the Colorado Rockies, in the winter of 1959 and was greeted by subzero temperatures. The camp, World War II training home for the Army's 10th Mountain Division, had not been used for years. It had been all but abandoned, with many of its buildings torn down. Several hastily constructed Quonset huts (prefabricated structures of corrugated, galvanized steel in a semicircular shape) in the northeast corner of the camp constituted our living and training area. The Tibetans called the place "dumra," which in Tibetan meant garden spot. The Colorado location, with its high snow-covered mountains reminded them of Tibet.

Security surrounding the Tibetan training program was tight. The Tibetans were flown secretly into Peterson Field (a military installation which at that time shared a runway with the city of Colorado Springs). Attired in U. S. Army fatigue uniforms, they were loaded into buses with blacked-out windows and driven in darkness west on U.S. Highway 24 into the mountains and Camp Hale. This procedure was repeated in reverse once each group of Tibetans had completed training. Few personnel had been cleared for the project, so we instructors had to double up as bus drivers, snow plow operators, and carry out other administrative and logistical functions. Our section of Camp Hale, marked as a facility belonging to Defense Department's Atomic Support Agency, was patrolled by a platoon of military police detailed from Fort Carson, the Army post near Colorado Springs. Signs everywhere proclaimed that no photographs were to be taken, and the military police immediately confronted any onlooker using a camera. I recall that on one of my visits to Leadville, the nearest town, I was asked where I worked. When I responded Camp Hale, the questioner then said: "Oh, you're the people who are burying atomic bombs in the mountains." We left it at that. I would spend almost three years in a Quonset hut at Camp Hale, with a few interruptions when I accompanied the Tibetans to Okinawa, Saipan, or Thailand.

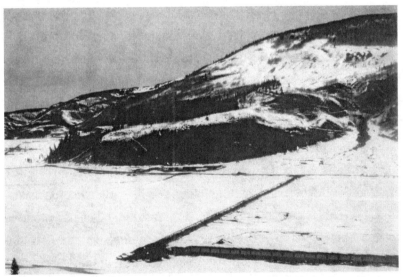

Snow-covered and abandoned Camp Hale site. The Tibetans called it "Dumra"—garden spot. Author's personal collection)

The training program for each group of Tibetans was scheduled to last four-to-six weeks, but was often extended, awaiting the State Department's obtaining overflight permission from the governments of Pakistan and India. Overflying those two countries was necessary to insert the Tibetans by parachute into Tibet and Nepal and then to keep them supplied. During their training, the Tibetans received instruction in clandestine operations, explosives, modern weaponry, small-unit tactics, parachuting (including actual jumps from an aircraft), and other military skills, especially map reading. They were also taught how to organize an underground network; how to conduct radio operations, including coding; and how to hide weapons and supplies. In addition to explosives, their weapons training in both U.S. and foreign models ranged from small arms to the U.S. 75-mm. recoilless rifle. The Tibetans were all excellent marksmen, exceptionally accurate with the recoilless rifle. One of their favorite weapons was the British Sten gun because it was light and capable of a high rate of fire. We used live ammunition during weapons field training, and fortunately (to my surprise) never experienced any mishaps. In all of our presentations on military tactics, which included ambush techniques and diversionary operations, we stressed to the Tibetans that they should strike fast and furious, but then flee. We emphasized that they should not engage the Chinese in lengthy firefights.

Training the Tibetans proved to be easier than I had envisioned. Since almost all of them could not speak English, we relied on exceptionally capable Tibetan interpreters. Prompted mainly by their hatred for the Chinese who were oppressing their countrymen, the Tibetans were ready and eager to learn. They were truly mountain people who possessed tremendous lower body strength, and could walk for long distances uphill with heavy loads on their backs almost effortlessly. Some of the Tibetans that I taught were Khampa warriors who had accompanied the Dalai Lama on his escape from Lhasa and were known for their horsemanship and physical strength. I knew them to be fierce warriors who would passionately defend their religion and the Dalai Lama to the death. Interestingly, a few monks were part of each group of trainees.

Rare photo of Tibetan Freedom Fighters at Camp Hale, ca. 1961.
(Courtesy Hoover Institution Archives, Stanford University)

Although Camp Hale was not being used, the Army still maintained control. This worked to our advantage since we received most of our logistical support from Fort Carson. For example, some of our medical problems—broken bones, serious cuts and abrasions, and tapeworms—were treated at the post hospital. We also used Fort Carson's airfield, known as Butts Field, for most of our parachute training. The Tibetans had to make three jumps prior to completing the course at Camp Hale. These were intended not only to familiarize the trainee with parachuting techniques but also to give him confidence. In all my years with the Agency I never heard of any Tibetan who refused to jump, or, for that matter, resist reinfiltration into Tibet. My impression, shared by all of the Camp Hale instructors, was that they were anxious to return to their homeland to fight the hated Chinese oppressors.

At one point during one of the training courses, we received word from headquarters that the Tibetans being resupplied by air were not clearing the drop zone of supplies fast enough. The Agency recommended that our training include the use of pack animals such as mules to speed up removal of air-dropped cargo. We canvassed the entire country and found that although Fort Carson once had a mule-packing school, it had closed down. We discovered, however, that mule-packing was part of one of the Marine Corps courses at Quantico. Consequently, we took a group of about a dozen Tibetans to the Marine base. I was excited about this change of pace not only because of my background as a Marine, but also because there would be an opportunity for the Tibetans to learn something about Marine Corps small unit tactics. The Marine instructors, using our translators, put the Tibetans through two weeks of intensive training. It included the pack-mule course where the emphasis was on transporting the 75-mm. recoilless rifle, and instruction in small unit tactics, which reinforced our emphasis on "hit-and-run" and overcoming the Tibetans' tendency to stand and fight. Throughout the training at Quantico, the Marine instructors were not aware of the students' nationality. I remember that one day an old gunnery sergeant asked me who they were. I replied, "Who do you think they are?" He quickly responded: "North Koreans." I didn't contradict him. The "Gunny" also confided in me that the students actually knew more about packing animals than he did. He had no idea he was attempting to train mountain people who had packed yaks and ponies all their lives!

We never smoked in front of our trainees, although a few instructors smoked in their own living quarters. I noticed that many of the Tibetans, including the interpreters, used snuff which they inhaled through their nose. I had used Copenhagen chewing tobacco in my college days as a member of a football team made up of ex-blue collar steel workers from the Pittsburgh area. After coming into contact with some "smoke jumpers" (forest fire fighters) near Camp Hale, I had begun to use it again, particularly on field exercises. Soon, several of our interpreters began to use it in place of snuff. Its use grew rapidly, and I found myself buying rolls of Copenhagen for our trainees. One story suggests how much the Tibetans had become attached to chewing tobacco. We had not heard for a long time from a team we had sent into Tibet, and were worried. Eventually they made a radio broadcast. They didn't ask for ammo or grenades—they asked for six rolls of Copenhagen!

Author at "Dumra". (Author's personal collection)

We were not often able to find out whether our training program had been effective. On one occasion, however, we learned that in ambushing a Chinese convoy, a group of Camp Hale-trained Tibetans recovered a number of documents, contained in a bloody pouch taken from one of the dead Chinese that turned out to be extremely important. These materials included information on the Chinese order of battle, Communist Party directives, references to personnel changes in the party, PLA journals, and instructions that the Tibetan resistance fighters and their supporters were to be totally eliminated. The pouch and its contents were immediately sent back to Washington. Agency analysts described recovery of the materials as one of the best intelligence coups since the Korean War. When translated, the PLA documents revealed:

1. That Mao Tse-tung's Great Leap Forward was a failure, with disastrous consequences for the Chinese economy.
2. The severity of the Sino-Soviet rift and its implications for international communism.
3. The weakness of the PLA, belying its status as a signifcant component of the Chinese order of battle.

There is an oil painting mounted on the wall of the Intelligence Art Gallery in the original CIA headquarters building (a new addition to the headquarters opened in 1991) at Langley, Virginia, that depicts the ambush described above. The painting, by Keith Woodcock, is entitled, *The Secret PLA Pouch Heads for K Building.* We Camp Hale veterans take great satisfaction from this famous ambush knowing that it was initiated and executed by Tibetans we had trained.

"The secret PLA pouch heads for K Building" [CIA Headquarters].
(Copyright © Keith Woodcock, artist. Used by permission.)

I mentioned that I sometimes accompanied the Tibetans to overseas locations. One of those trips, supposed to last only a few weeks, turned into a trying, months-long ordeal, particularly for the Tibetans. As the Tibetan resistance grew, the Chinese sent heavy concentrations of soldiers into eastern Tibet. The resistance leaders then moved their main base of operations to north central Nepal on Tibet's southern border, known as the Mustang ("fertile plain"). The guerilla fighters operating out of this area were having some successes, and C-130 airlifts were keeping them supplied. The Agency was pleased. But back at Camp Hale we had about fifteen Tibetan resistance fighters from the Mustang area who were eager to return to their homeland and reenter the fight.

Very late on the night of December 6, 1961, I got behind the wheel of an Army bus with blackened windows and loaded our energetic and excited trainees. As we had done several times in the past, we planned to arrive at Peterson Field by 6:00 a.m. A C-124 aircraft would be waiting to board us, hopefully well before most of Colorado Springs awoke. We were accompanied by a squad of military police. Unfortunately, the weather worked against us. The snow-packed roads caused delays, and I was forced to make two long stops along the way. As a result, we arrived about two hours behind schedule. By that time, approximately sixty-five employees of the Kensair Corporation had arrived for work in a company hangar adjacent to our parked and waiting C-124. Prior to debarking the Tibetans from the bus to board the aircraft, our military police escort was directed to ensure the secrecy of the transfer. The over-eager military police not only detained all the Kensair employees in the hangar, but also rounded up other workers in the vicinity and herded them into the building—at gunpoint. To complicate the situation further, the sheriff of El Paso County and two of his deputies who had responded to reports of some kind of disturbance were prevented from entering the airport. The military police explained to them that the C-124 was being loaded with classified material. Eventually, despite all this turmoil, we managed to depart Peterson Field with our Tibetans.

The following day an article appeared in the Colorado Springs *Gazette Telegraph* with the headline: "Gestapo Tactics at Peterson Field Bring Apology from Army." The article noted that forty-five "Orientals" had been spotted in military uniforms entering a military transport aircraft at the field. It further stated that the "Orientals" had disembarked from a bus with curtains over the windows. Numerous apologies came from Army officials at Fort Carson and from the Army's chief of information in Washington, D.C. Soon the wire services picked up the story, and inquiries were made to the Office of the Secretary of Defense. A spokesman for then-Secretary of Defense Robert McNamara confided in the journalists, explained what was going on at Camp Hale, and pleaded for them to drop the story, which they agreed to do. Fortunately, after about a week or so, interest in the incident died away.

Meanwhile the Tibetans and I, onboard the C-124, made our way to Okinawa with refueling stops at McClellan Air Force Base in California, and Hickam Air Force Base in Hawaii. Okinawa was supposed to be a brief transit stop on the way to Pakistan but, unfortunately, because of a conflict between Pakistan and India that soured U.S. relations with the Pakistanis, overflight rights were in jeopardy. We decided to wait out the situation at the CIA complex on Saipan. Its cover name was the "Naval Technical Training Unit," and was very secure. It would be our home for many months as we waited for U. S. relations with Pakistan to improve.

Upon arrival on Saipan the Tibetans and I were assigned to a remote area located in the northernmost part of the island. Saipan had been the scene of one of the bloodiest battles (June-July 1944) in the Pacific in World War II. This was evident to me and, especially, the Tibetans when we viewed firsthand the metallic carnage left over from the battle. We saw rusting hulks of ships offshore, bullet-riddled tanks, crumbling command posts, and even some uniform remnants. We were quartered in the Marpi Point area of the island, and from there had access to Suicide Cliff and Banzai Cliff where thousands of Japanese soldiers and civilians had leaped to their deaths. Japanese propaganda had caused them to fear that they would be brutally treated by their American conquerors.

To keep the Tibetans occupied productively, I set up the semblance of a training program. I asked them what subjects from the course at Camp Hale they would like reemphasized and reinforced. With the help of Agency personnel on Saipan and with some modifications, I was able to repeat parts of their training program. The Tibetans all wanted to learn to drive a jeep, so I requisitioned a couple of jeeps and proceeded to present my version of driver training. I also introduced them to the gasoline engine—at least what I knew about it. We never did take an engine apart because I wouldn't have known how to put it back together, but they all enjoyed the experience. I also continued the physical education program begun at Camp Hale with morning physical training sessions.

The CIA staff in the "Naval Technical Training Unit" on Saipan was extremely helpful, providing me and my Tibetans with any assistance requested. The staff also saw to it that we had movies and taped television westerns for entertainment. A favorite of the group was the long-running television series, *Cheyenne*, starring Clint Walker. The Tibetans liked it so much that they began to imitate Walker's mannerisms.

Once on Saipan I discovered that I was responsible for furnishing my group with three meals a day. Fortunately, the Agency's dining facility supplied the evening meal, but I had to come up with breakfast and lunch. My culinary skills were limited, so I improvised as best I could. Breakfast always consisted of dry cereal, toast, and coffee or tea. Once in a while I made hot oatmeal. Lunch was luncheon meats, cheese, bread, and a variety of condiments, and, again, coffee or tea. No one complained (at least not to my face), so I had apparently succeeded in pulling off my culinary deception.

One day, the CIA's chief of station on Saipan notified me that they had received a cable indicating that I should contact my home in Pennsylvania. Although the cable stressed that it was not an emergency, I began to imagine all sorts of situations—all bad! The chief of station also told me that he had arranged for a Navy aircraft to fly me to Guam where I could use a radio relay system to contact home. I rushed to the air station, boarded the aircraft, and was off to Guam. While en route, my imagination again tormented me. As soon as we landed, I made my way to the radio relay station and telephoned home. My mother answered and, after a few pleasantries, I asked her what was wrong. She replied "I have no wall space." Agitated, I said "wall space, wall space, I don't understand." Almost in pain, she said that "the fireplace takes up too much wall space." Then it dawned on me. I was building a new house for my parents and my mother was dissatisfied with the amount of wall space taken up by the new fireplace. Upon realizing my mother's dilemma, I told her to seal up the fireplace. She appeared to be pleased with that solution to her problem. After exchanging a few more pleasantries we ended the call, and I immediately returned by Navy aircraft to Saipan. After arriving, I thanked the chief of station for his courtesy. He inquired if everything was ok at home. I told him and others on his staff that it was a personal family matter that had been corrected. I figured this was the best way to describe the situation. Surely no one would believe the wall space story.

Weeks stretched into months on Saipan. My students were overtrained and rapidly becoming overstayed. I organized them into search parties to hunt for World War II artifacts. We also attempted to shoot sand sharks off Marpi Point—anything to pass the time. Our extended stay did not seem to have any adverse effects on the Tibetans' enthusiasm, although they repeatedly asked when they would be able to rejoin their countrymen in the Mustang area. My often repeated answer was: once overflight permission was obtained from Pakistan. Through the Agency's chief of station in Saipan we cabled CIA headquarters, advising of the plight of our

Tibetans. Headquarters was aware of the situation and told us that negotiations were underway not only with Pakistan but also with India for permission to overfly the two countries to parachute and resupply the resistance fighters.

Finally, after months of waiting, our group left Saipan by air for Takhli Royal Thai Air Base in Thailand en route to India and Pakistan. Here I rendezvoused with Roger McCarthy, who was still head of the CIA's Tibetan project. McCarthy was very much respected by the Tibetans; he, in turn, always showed them similar respect, describing them as brave, honest, and loyal warriors. Before their departure from Thailand, McCarthy gave the Tibetans a final briefing. I'm sure he thought that that this might be the last group that we would be able to re-infiltrate, and felt compelled to make the send-off memorable. I recall that it was a very somber moment. McCarthy extolled the Tibetans' determination to fight the hated enemy—the Chinese. He complimented them for their patience during their long stay on Saipan, attributing the delay to the discord between Pakistan and India. He wished them well, again thanking them for their perseverance. He then removed a large pill from a container. He held it up and called it the "lethal pill"—a cyanide ampoule that he said was only to be used when death was imminent. He related that it was up to the individual whether to use the pill. He went on to say that once you put it in your mouth (at this point he popped the ampoule he was holding into his mouth and continued), you had to mash down on it to release the cyanide. According to him, once the pill was activated and ingested, death would occur in two-to-three seconds. I can assure you McCarthy did not mash down on the ampoule, but I was nonetheless startled when he thrust it into his mouth! I had never seen anyone do that in all my years with the Agency. After the briefing, which amounted to a great deal of handshaking and backslapping, the group was taken to the waiting aircraft. Shortly thereafter, the Tibetans were on their way to their final destination.

McCarthy and I parted after the Tibetans left Thailand. I flew to Kadena, Okinawa, and, after a short stay, returned to Camp Hale. Many changes had taken place at the camp. Most of the instructors had been reassigned, and the camp was being operated by a skeleton crew. There was a great deal of talk about closing down the task force altogether. After a few days in the semi-deserted camp I received notification from headquarters that I was to report for training in the Agency's Junior Officer Training Program (JOT) in Washington, D.C. The JOT program's purpose was to train case officers (an agent assigned responsibility for a particular project) for the Agency, and it was highly selective. I felt very good about being chosen, and was sure McCarthy had recommended me.

CHAPTER 5

FROM CIA TO FBI

Prior to reporting to Washington to enroll in the CIA's Junior Officer Training Program (JOT), I spent several weeks with my family in Old Forge. My father had little use for my employment with the CIA. He always wanted me to go into the FBI. When asked, "Who does Don work for?" he would respond facetiously, "I don't know—the AFL-CIO, some labor organization." He, of course, knew that I worked for the CIA, but always put it down.

After a few weeks in Old Forge, I reported in late November 1962 to CIA headquarters in Washington. At that time, the Agency was in the process of moving to Langley but still occupied the various temporary buildings I have previously described. I settled into a small apartment on the third floor of a three-story brownstone on Massachusetts Avenue. I enjoyed my return to headquarters and became acquainted with many case officers who were our instructors in the JOT Program. Their fascinating presentations, drawn from their personal experiences, gave a clear and concise overview of the Agency's activities throughout the world. The presentations covering Africa indicated that there was little Agency activity in the central and eastern parts of the continent, but more in the north and south. This observation piqued my interest. I had been reading several books on Africa by Robert Ruark and especially liked *Uhuru* and also *Something of Value*. Both were interesting and informative, and further excited me about this part of the world. I learned that one of the predominant languages in East Africa was Italian—a hangover from Italy's occupation of the area before World War II. I felt somewhat familiar with Italian as my grandparents, who had emigrated from Italy, spoke it to our family.

Armed with my newly acquired knowledge of Africa and my strong desire to see the continent, I approached our course director and asked if I could request an assignment there after completing the JOT Program. I explained to him my reasons for desiring this duty. He replied that he would make my request known to the proper officials. After a short time, he contacted me and said that since I had been sponsored by the Far East Division to attend JOT, I was slated to return to them. It looked like I would be assigned to the Agency's station in Bangkok, Thailand. This did not sit well with me; I did not want to return to East Asia. As a result of this news, I did a great deal of soul searching that included a few calls to my father. He once again stated that I should "go with the Bureau." After several weeks of evaluating my position within the Agency, I decided to resign. It was a difficult decision because I had truly enjoyed my assignments and the many friends I had made in both the Security Division and the Far East Division. It was hard to turn my back on an organization for which I had so much respect, but I was now determined to get into the FBI.

After I resigned, I concentrated my attention on a pretty X-ray technician, named Jan Paripovich, whom I had met at the Fort Carson hospital while I was involved with parachute training for the Tibetans. I hoped she had good memories of me; I had been impressed not only with her beauty but her intellect as well. I remembered that our first meeting had presented me with a dilemma. I told her I would pick her up at the hospital, and we would join a group at the Officers Club. Unfortunately, my only transportation was either an Army ambulance or the sixty-passenger bus with blacked-out windows. I settled for the ambulance. Jan, thinking this was some sort of gag, went along with my "medical chariot" approach to our first date. I knew that this beautiful young woman, surrounded by thousands of soldiers, would not stay single for long. So I acted fast following my resignation from the CIA. After clearing out of my apartment in Washington, I flew to Colorado. To my surprise and great joy, Jan was happy to see me and our relationship blossomed. We were married on March 3, 1962 in Colorado Springs. Jan is of Serbian descent and possessed of a fiercely loving nature that contributed much to our marriage and to my professional life. We would be blessed with two children, Jon who was born while we were in Mississippi, and Ann, born after we returned to Colorado.

After we were married, Jan and I remained in Colorado Springs for several months. During this period, I was jobless. Fortunately Jan, who continued her work as an X-ray technician, could support both of us. While we were in Colorado Springs, I heard that the FBI was soliciting applications. When I informed several of my Agency friends that I planned to apply to be a special agent with the FBI, they were not very encouraging. They explained that the Bureau and J. Edgar Hoover, its legendary director, were still irritated over the large number of agents that had left the Bureau for the CIA when the new intelligence agency was established in 1947. Undeterred, I decided to apply to the Bureau through its Philadelphia office. I felt that my father's having been a police chief in eastern Pennsylvania would enhance my chances of being selected. In retrospect, I don't think my father's status had any influence because almost eight months went by before I received any word about my application, my test results, or my interview. I now think that my overseas assignments with the CIA, which lengthened the time required for the FBI to complete a background investigation, caused the delay. Finally, I was informed by letter that I was to report to the Justice Department Building in Washington on February 25, 1963, to be sworn in as a new agent.

When I received the letter, Jan and I were residing with my parents in Pennsylvania. I recall that eventful day very vividly. My father retrieved the mail and yelled upstairs to me that there was a letter for me from the FBI. I had just stepped out of the shower and yelled back for him to open it. After a few seconds, he shouted back his congratulations and the comment, "At last you have a man's job!" My father was also impressed that Director Hoover had signed the letter. In fact he continued to extol the Bureau—the premier law enforcement agency in the world—and emphasized the many benefits of working for it

In Washington, Jan and I rented an apartment in the Georgetown section. As directed, at 9:00 a.m. on February 25, 1963, I reported to Room 5231 of the Justice Department Building and took my oath of office. I was now in the FBI and a member of New Agents Class No. 7, which consisted of twenty-two individuals with varied backgrounds, but all sharing a desire to become full-fledged agents. Most of my classmates hailed from the East Coast (many from New York City); only a few were from the western part of the country. We would be together as new agents in training for fourteen weeks. Most of the instruction took place on the 6th floor of the Old Post Office Building (now a tourist attraction) located at 12th and Pennsylvania, next to the Justice Department Building. Our instructors were very experienced senior agents. Their presentations were detailed and intensive, and covered federal criminal procedures, Bureau rules and regulations, and interview and interrogation techniques. We also took report-writing classes, and became familiar with various methods of internal Bureau communications. Additionally, we participated in moot court sessions to learn how to testify. One of the lasting impressions I took from these sessions was that when testifying one should always wear high socks. The instructor explained that exposing the bare skin of your leg while on the stand, would detract from your testimony. I can assure you that I always wore high socks when I testified in any court, especially in Federal District Court!

Our training also consisted of three, one-week periods at the FBI Academy, located on the Marine Corps base at Quantico. (In 1972, a new facility, also at Quantico, replaced the original Academy that I attended in 1963.) At Quantico we had a minimum of classroom time, but heavy concentrations of field work. We fired and qualified on all the weapons in the Bureau's inventory—shotguns, rifles, submachine guns, and, of course, the .38 caliber revolvers that each agent carried. We also spent lots of time on arrest techniques and in physical activities, including self-defense techniques, boxing, and some judo training. Additionally, we participated in several practical exercises, such as simulated bank robberies, extortions, and kidnappings.

During my training I was interviewed by two assistant directors and several instructors, all wanting to know why I had resigned from the CIA. My answer was that I had wanted to be an FBI agent since my early boyhood, and that my entry into the CIA stemmed from a desire for adventure, coupled with a flattering recommendation by a former OSS officer. In addition, I related to my inquisitors that my father was a former chief of police and always told me that if I wanted to go into law enforcement, I should go with the FBI.

While at the Academy, we regularly attended a local pub known as the Globe and Anchor, operated by retired Marine Corps Maj. Rick Spooner and his wife, Gloria. After our evening meal, we

were allowed to leave the Academy and go to town, but were required to return no later than 10:00 p.m., at which time all Academy doors were locked. It was always a race against time to gulp down a beer or two at the Globe and Anchor, discuss the events of the day, and beat the lockdown. Many times the major, or his wife, would pile members of our new agents' class into their station wagon and deposit us at the Academy just in time to

The FBI Badge

avoid our being locked out.

After our last week in Quantico, we returned to Washington to complete the final phase of our training, which included a series of examinations. The word leaked out: All twenty-two members of New Agents Class No. 7 had successfully completed the course.

There wasn't much of a graduation ceremony to mark our achieving the rank of special agent, except that following it, Director Hoover met with us, shaking our hands as we passed by in a line. Afterwards our class picture was taken, and our first assignments announced. It appeared to me that many of the class members from the East Coast were assigned to offices in the Midwest or South; and those of us, like me, who wanted an assignment in the West, received one. I hoped for the Houston office but was assigned to Dallas. Wherever our assignments, we all believed that the future as a special agent with the FBI was bright and limitless. We were eager and anxious to get going. That we were in fact special agents hit home when we were issued our credentials and our .38 caliber revolvers.

Graduation photo, FBI New Agents Class No. 7, 1963.
Author in second row, third from right. (Author's personal collection)

While I was in training, friends in Washington kept my 1962 Corvette in their garage because I did not want to park it in the street near our apartment. Jan and I used it whenever possible to visit historical sites in the Washington area. The Corvette was equipped with a stick shift and Jan was not good at using it; as a result, she refused to drive the car. Soon after we received our orders for Dallas she adamantly insisted that we trade in the Corvette for an air-conditioned sedan. She commented that she did not want to live in Dallas without an air-conditioned vehicle. But I felt the real reason for her insisting that we get rid of the Corvette was the stick shift. And so I parted with the car, one of my treasures.

Air-conditioned automobiles were not that common in 1963. When we arrived in eastern Pennsylvania to spend a few days with my parents, en route to Dallas, my father looked over our new car. Surprised when told that it was air-conditioned, he said, "The only cars around here that are air-conditioned belong to the funeral directors." A few days later Jan and I set out for Dallas, quite comfortable in our air-conditioned sedan.

CHAPTER 6

BIG D AND AMARILLO

We arrived in Dallas in late May 1963 and, with the assistance of the FBI's Dallas office, obtained an apartment in the Love Field section of the city. Jan and I were eager to begin our stay. We knew that Bureau rules called for a "first office agent," which I was, to remain in that office for at least two years and then move on to his next assignment. The thought of spending time in Dallas was appealing.

Although historically a frontier town, by the early 1960s Dallas was a bustling business center with a future that seemed unlimited. Jan had attended several Cotton Bowl games there with friends and was impressed with the enthusiasm and good nature of the Texans. Everything seemed to be bigger in Texas. She was also impressed with the opportunities for shopping, especially at Neiman-Marcus. My impression of Dallas, garnered after a few weeks on the job, was that it was a Southern city heavily involved in Democratic Party politics, yet divided over the current Kennedy administration.

Blacks favored the Kennedys; whites were generally critical. In our associations with our non-Bureau friends who resided in our apartment building, I was amazed by their ferocious desire to make their fortunes as soon as possible. It was more than fierce determination—it was an obsession.

Jan and our car while we were en route to my first FBI assignment in Dallas, Texas. (Author's personal collection)

Once settled, I looked forward to working in the city. The FBI's Dallas office had a reputation as a good, solid field office which had successfully investigated some of the Bureau's most important cases. Many of the field office's agents were former law enforcement officers, judges, and state officials from both Texas and Oklahoma who had resigned their positions to join the FBI. They comprised what was called the "palace guard"—veteran agents who usually smoked cigars, handled all the important cases, and constituted the backbone of the field office. Along with their supervisors, they took it upon themselves to maintain the Bureau's positive, "pure-as-the-driven-snow" image. On the day I reported, I was wearing a blue shirt; one of the supervisors quickly admonished that I was to wear the Bureau's traditional attire—a white shirt.

As a first office agent, I rotated through a variety of assignments. In each, I was teamed with experienced agents, accompanying them and observing their work. Initially, I was paired with Jim Hosty who would later become one of the lead agents working the Kennedy assassination. At the time I was associated with Hosty, he was handling most of the intelligence matters for the Dallas office. We worked several intelligence cases together, but none involved the soon to be infamous Lee Harvey Oswald.

My next assignment, to the major case squad, was a humbling experience. That squad handled bank robberies, extortions, and kidnappings, and was composed mainly of senior agents of the palace guard. While I was assigned to the major case squad, a bank robbery occurred. Two individuals had held up the bank tellers at gunpoint and had gotten away with cash. The bank was located next to a parking garage where they had hidden their getaway car. They successfully exited the garage, but were stopped a short distance away and arrested by the Dallas police. The stolen money was not with them. We began an intensive search along their escape route. Since I was the new guy, I was assigned the inglorious task of looking through the trash dumpsters located in the garage. I never found any of the loot, but instead incurred a large cleaning bill for a permanently-stained suit! The money was recovered; the robbers had pitched it out the window of the getaway car. Still searching the dumpsters, I was the last to be notified that it had been found.

I then spent a short and pleasant tour with the applicant squad. Its mission was to investigate the backgrounds of prospective FBI candidates. One of the applicant cases assigned to me involved an individual named Robert Joseph Binford. In connection with the case I had to conduct a neighborhood investigation; that is, inquire from the applicant's neighbors as to what kind of person he was and if they were aware of any problems. During my investigation, I contacted two neighbors who lived adjacent to Binford's residence. Both said they knew no one by that name. When I asked a third neighbor, the result was the same. He had not heard of Robert Joseph Binford either. I was exasperated and decided to examine the applicant's history more closely. Eureka! I found that he used an "aka" ("also known as") of "Bobbi Jo." I immediately recontacted the three neighbors; they *all* knew "Bobbi Jo Binford," and each recommended him highly for the position.

One of my most memorable experiences in Dallas occurred during my indoctrination into the fugitive squad, which handled the cases of individuals who were wanted by law enforcement for a variety of crimes, declared to be fugitives, and who were on the run. The squad was composed of several members of the palace guard and was an extremely tight bunch, its members well-liked by their counterparts in the Dallas Police Department. They were also known as the pranksters in the office. One day I accompanied several of them to the Dallas Police Department. After being introduced to and shaking hands with the uniformed Dallas police officers at the entry point, we made our way to the second floor, which was occupied by the detectives, or "Dicks." All of the windows in the police station were open and, although it was mid-morning, the Dallas heat was already oppressive. Apparently air-conditioning had not been an item in the department's budget for 1963. I was introduced to a lieutenant who was seated behind a desk, his back to the open window. He asked to see my credentials. As I was showing them to him, he abruptly snatched them from my hand, examined them indifferently, remarked that "These don't look like you," and tossed them out the open window. I was horrified! I couldn't believe that anyone would do something like that. Frantically I ran to the window and anxiously looked down. I saw an individual in a western-style Stetson waving a black object and smiling. I then became conscious of the laughter behind me and realized I was the butt of a joke. It was the kind known as "cop humor" that all law enforcement people enjoy, especially when at the expense of the FBI—not at the FBI as an institution but at the expense of the individual agent. The Dallas police officers present, along with some of the mischievous and complicit agents accompanying me, all had a good laugh.

After a period of indoctrination, I was permanently assigned to the applicant squad. Assignment to this unit was normal procedure in the Dallas office, and represented its effort to continue to familiarize a new agent with the city and its environs. I enjoyed my work with the new applicant squad and during that period, was also frequently called upon to assist in investigating numerous bank robberies and other major crimes.

In the late summer of 1963, Gordon Shanklin, the special agent in charge (SAC) of the Dallas office advised me that there was an opening in the Dallas office's Resident Agency in Amarillo, Texas. He wanted to know if I would be interested in relocating there. I told him I would like to discuss the move with Jan first, and Shanklin, a great boss, agreed. Amarillo was the largest city in the Texas panhandle (a part of the state Texans referred to as the "high plains"), and about an hour or so by car from the Oklahoma state line. The reassignment appealed to Jan as she was a Colorado native; the relocation would put us within a five-hour drive of her home in Pueblo, and she readily agreed to the move. The SAC was notified, and in early September we were on our way to Amarillo. Thus began a new phase in my career at the Bureau—that of resident agent.

During my years of service in the Bureau there were 59 field offices, most (unlike Dallas) located in state capitals. Scattered between them, and under their jurisdiction, were 516 smaller satellite offices called Resident Agencies (RAs) staffed by more than 2,200 resident agents. The RAs were necessary because most field offices encompassed areas too large to be covered from a single location.

J. Edgar Hoover did not particularly care for the RAs; he considered them to be a necessary evil—necessary because they covered large territories; and evil because they were too far away from FBI headquarters to control and supervise properly. In this regard, each resident agent in every RA was required to sign in daily on a register indicating the time he reported to work and to submit a report each day specifying how he spent every hour while on duty. In addition, the resident agent was required to submit a "three card," or locator card, which indicated his anticipated contacts and whereabouts that particular day.

Despite such bureaucratic requirements, I found the atmosphere in the Amarillo RA to be informal and relaxed. Realism took precedence over the rulebook. The Amarillo RA's territory was divided among the five resident agents. The senior agent was William Jenkins who had many years of experience in the Bureau and was responsible for investigating most violations of federal law in Amarillo itself. (William's brother was Walter Jenkins, the longtime aide to the then-Vice President Lyndon B. Johnson.) If the offense consisted of a major felony, such as bank robbery, extortion, or kidnapping, the entire RA assisted in the investigation. The assistant resident agent handled most of the stolen car cases for the Amarillo RA (a frequent occurrence since U. S. Route 66 ran through the city), and was also responsible for the agency's northwest sector to the New Mexico and Oklahoma state lines. The three remaining agents also had geographical responsibilities. One was responsible for the northeast sector to the Oklahoma state line, and another the southeast area of the panhandle. The southwest sector belonged to me. It extended from Amarillo to the New Mexico state line. In addition to their geographical responsibilities, all five agents worked on cases assigned by the Dallas office that concerned the Amarillo area.

My assignment to the Amarillo RA proved to be fortuitous. There I met Tom O'Maley, a wily and seasoned veteran of the Bureau with a solid reputation as an excellent report writer, or "paper man" in Bureau jargon. He was from Boston (local law enforcement officers laughed at his New England accent) and had been an Army intelligence officer before joining the FBI. O'Maley took me under his wing, and I spent as much time with him as I could, both on and off the job. He was a mentor of mine, and I emulated many of his traits throughout my career in the Bureau (especially in report writing).

Most of my duties in the Amarillo RA dealt with searching for parole and military selective service violators, deserters (the Vietnam War was going on at the time), and other fugitives. In addition, as I have mentioned, the entire RA responded in the event of a major crime. We all also had our share of what we referred to as "car cases"—vehicles stolen in another state and abandoned or recovered in our jurisdiction. Such cases came under the Dyer Act, a Bureau enforcement responsibility. All agents also shared in the high volume of security investigations, a result of the close proximity of the Pantex nuclear facility to Amarillo.

The southwestern sector of the Amarillo RA assigned to me included the counties of Randall, Deaf Smith, Parmer, and Swisher. I worked very diligently to get to know their law enforcement officials and to gain their confidence in a variety of ways. For example, whenever assigned an investigation in one of those counties, I always checked with local law enforcement before beginning my work and told them what I would be doing in their jurisdiction. More often than not, they would volunteer to assist me. Additionally, whenever I went to one of the counties, I made a point of having lunch or coffee with the local law enforcement personnel. In all of my dealings with them, I kept in mind what my father had always emphasized—that law enforcement was a two-way street—whatever assistance one received should not only be acknowledged but also repaid if possible. I diligently sought to follow this rule throughout my career and it served me well.

On one occasion while at Amarillo, I recall receiving a case from the Dallas office involving a deserter from Canyon in Randall County. On my next trip to Canyon I contacted one of my favorite Randall County deputies—I'll call him "Slim." He was a former Marine, and we spent much time talking about the Corps. Slim was appalled to learn that he knew the deserter and his family. Since he was familiar with the family, I asked Slim to accompany me to interview the deserter's parents in an attempt to locate their son's whereabouts. Slim readily agreed, adding that the parents of the deserter were good people and would cooperate. Slim and I traveled to a small ranch located on the outskirts of Canyon. As we approached the ranch house in a Randall County sheriff's vehicle, an elderly gentleman greeted us and ushered us into the kitchen where we met his wife. He insisted that we have some ice tea, and we all sat around the kitchen table. Slim introduced me and said I was looking for their son who had gone on "unauthorized leave" from the service. (I had previously instructed Slim not to use the term "deserter" in the presence of the parents.) I then explained that their son, a young man, had made a bad decision and that it was in the best interest of all concerned that he be returned to military control. I further explained that all I wanted to do was to return him to the military where he would be adjudicated under the Uniform Code of Military Justice. I added that it was possible that he might not even have to spend the night in jail. Upon hearing this, the deserter's father looked to his wife quizzically, and she nodded affirmatively. The father then abruptly stood and, pointing his finger toward the ceiling, said quietly, "He's upstairs in his bedroom." Slim and I went upstairs and found the deserter hiding under his bed. We pulled him out, and Slim told the deserter in a soft voice to "act like a man." The young man did not offer any resistance, so I allowed him some time with his parents. After their tearful goodbyes, we whisked him off to the county jail to await pickup by military authorities.

There was another military deserter case in my experience at Amarillo that did not go so smoothly. It took place near Hereford in Deaf Smith County, part of my jurisdiction. Prior investigation had indicated that the deserter was located at his parents' home, a small ranch located outside of Hereford. I traveled to the parents' home several times. My Bureau car was easily identified as law enforcement because of its radio "whip" antenna. Each time I went to the front door of the house, someone would open it, and two large, vicious, barking dogs would force me back into my vehicle. Several times the dogs would be unleashed even before I had gotten out of the car. This situation went on for several days and I was frustrated. Finally, in desperation, I sought help from my friend Pete, a Deaf Smith County sheriff's deputy. Over a cup of coffee I explained my unusual predicament. Pete said he knew the people in question and said they were tenants on the ranch. He enthusiastically agreed to help me and we traveled together to the ranch in my Bureau car. As soon as we arrived, Pete opened the passenger door, withdrew his side arm, took aim at the two attacking dogs, and shot them both. This all happened within a few seconds. I was stunned. A short time after the two shots were fired, the front door of the house opened wide and the young deserter appeared with his hands in the air. Very cautiously he walked to my car. I handcuffed him and placed him in the back seat. Pete then visited briefly with the family and we drove away to book the deserter into the county jail with instructions to hold him for military authorities. On the drive back, Pete told me what he had said to the deserter's father. He told him that if the family had cooperated, the whole incident could have been avoided.

In spite of the many regulations imposed on it, the RA represented the informal, relaxed side of the Bureau. Moreover, because of their close contact with the community, resident agents could call upon local law enforcement officials and other community leaders for help with their cases. I valued and enjoyed this kind of atmosphere. But the relative tranquility I experienced as a resident agent in Amarillo would soon be disturbed and my time there interrupted by a momentous event.

CHAPTER 7

THE KENNEDY ASSASSINATION

arly on a bright Friday afternoon in late November 1963, while traveling from Hereford to Canyon, I heard the news bulletin that both President John F. Kennedy and Governor John B. Connally of Texas had been shot in a motorcade in downtown Dallas in an open automobile. I was shocked when I heard the news and immediately pulled the Bureau car over to the side of the highway. I thought to myself, "My God, who would shoot the president of the United States and why?" How could the shooter manage to get by the top police and security personnel assigned to the president? For the time being, those questions would remain unanswered as I decided to forgo my stop in Canyon and return immediately to the RA in Amarillo.

When I arrived at the garage in Amarillo where we kept our Bureau cars, I saw a large group huddled around a radio and a television in the garage attendant's office. Included in the group were agents from the RA who had heard of the assassination and immediately returned from their assignments to the agency office. Everyone gathered there, including my fellow agents, were aghast and could not believe the dreadful news flash. We heard that President Kennedy died at 1:00 p.m. Central Time. We all then returned to the RA office, which was located on the second floor of Amarillo's main post office down the street from the garage. We waited late into the evening, thinking there might be some requests or orders from the Dallas field office. But nothing was forthcoming. We then returned to our residences and experienced the shocking tragedy with our families.

Jack Ruby shooting Lee Harvey Oswald in basement of Dallas Police Station, November 24, 1963. (Photo by and copyright © Bob Jackson. Used by permission)

During the weekend, all of the resident agents continued to keep in close contact, still anticipating some assignment or request from the Dallas office. We were aware through FBI agents there that an individual known as Lee Harvey Oswald, the alleged shooter, had been arrested eighty minutes after Kennedy was shot. Additionally J.D. Tippit, a Dallas patrolman, had been shot and killed, also allegedly by Oswald. Further, Vice President Johnson had been sworn in as president; and prior to flying to Washington, had phoned J. Edgar Hoover and ordered a full investigation. Hoover, according to the Dallas office, then ordered an inspector and thirty agents to Dallas. We discussed this at length within the RA and decided that still more agents would be required for the investigation, especially to determine whether it was a widespread conspiracy.

Then a stunning turn of events made certain that additional investigators would be needed. Jack Ruby, a Dallas nightclub owner, shot and killed Oswald while he was being transferred from the Dallas city jail to the county jail. The entire country watched the shooting on television. We heard that President Johnson had immediately ordered the Bureau to expand its probe to include any possible connection between Ruby and Oswald. The Amarillo RA continued to await orders, and soon the call came from Dallas requesting that it send two of its most senior agents to Dallas on temporary duty. This request excluded me, and I was disappointed. My disappointment lasted only a short time, however, as I was soon on a commercial flight from Amarillo to Dallas. Needless to say, I was excited to be able to participate in an investigation of such historical importance.

Upon arriving in Dallas I immediately reported to my supervisor, who instructed me to report to the surveillance group responsible for Oswald's wife, Marina. In the early days following the assassination, the Bureau, in its effort to determine whether a conspiracy existed, imposed twenty-four-hour surveillance on every individual known to be connected to Oswald.

Once in Dallas, I learned much more about the man everyone now believed had killed President Kennedy. Oswald was described to me as a malcontent who claimed to be a Marxist. He had been in the Marines, learned to fire the M1 rifle, and was rated a sharpshooter on the Corps' ascending marksman/sharpshooter/expert scale. In 1959, he had renounced his U.S. citizenship and traveled to the Soviet Union where he was employed in a factory in Minsk, the capital and largest city of the then-Belorussian Soviet Socialist Republic. There he met Marina Nikolaevna Prusakova, a pharmacist, and they were married on April 30, 1961. Oswald soon became disillusioned with life under communism, and had his U.S. citizenship reinstated by the Department of State. He and Marina received permission from Soviet authorities to leave the Soviet Union together, and on June 1, 1962 traveled with their firstborn to the United States. They initially resided with relatives (his mother and brother) in Fort Worth, Texas. Bureau agents interviewed Oswald twice in August 1962. Both times he denied that he was involved in Soviet intelligence activities and said he would notify the FBI if the Soviets contacted him. The FBI interviewers described Oswald as belligerent and unwilling to discuss why he went to the Soviet Union or why he left. Based on the two interviews and extensive background investigations, the Bureau labeled Oswald's file "pending inactive" because, at that time, it had no reason to believe he was a spy, saboteur, or potential assassin.

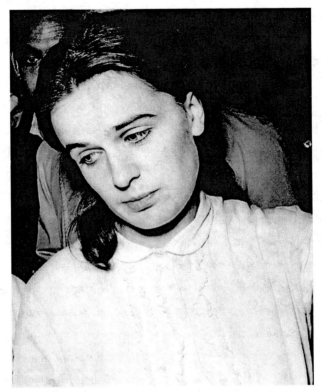

Marina Oswald at initial interview with Dallas police.
(Photo by and copyright © Bob Jackson. Used by permission)

My initial assignment in the Kennedy assassination investigation was to the surveillance team directly observing the actions and contacts of Marina Oswald during the nighttime hours. It was a real disappointment; I had hoped for something more glamorous. But it should have been expected. Not only was I a first office agent but also one with only a few months experience in the Bureau—a rookie for all practical purposes. At the time of the assassination, Marina was living in Irving, a suburb of Dallas, with Mrs. Ruth Paine, perhaps the best friend Marina and her two young children ever had. I was told that the relationship between Marina and her husband had begun to deteriorate after they arrived in the United States. Numerous arguments occurred, and Oswald, who possessed a hot temper that sometimes sent him into rages, physically abused Marina. Paine witnessed this abuse and sympathized with Marina—so much so that she allowed Marina and her two children to reside with her in her four-bedroom home in Irving. Their relationship was very close; they were both young mothers who talked about families and housework. It was further strengthened by the fact that Paine, who had studied Russian, used Marina to improve her Russian. In turn, Marina learned English from Paine. On one occasion, before Marina and her children moved into her home, Paine drove them to New Orleans to join Oswald for a short period. Paine disliked Lee Harvey Oswald and, although she allowed him to visit Marina and the children on weekends, he could not stay overnight. She felt that Oswald was haughty, arrogant, and insolent, an impression shared by members of the small Russian community in the Dallas-Fort Worth area who helped Marina and her children with food, clothing, and other necessities.

As I have mentioned, my assignment was nighttime surveillance of Marina Oswald. Since she had moved into Ruth Paine's home, this meant staking out the Paine residence from 7 p.m. to 7 a.m. There was very little activity at the residence during those hours. In fact, neither of the women ventured outside of the home at night while I was on duty. The few vehicles we observed turned out to belong to friends from the small Russian-speaking community who aided Marina and her children. We attributed the lack of activity to Marina's and Ruth Paine's routine as young mothers. The Irving Police Department was well aware of our surveillance; they would often ride by and acknowledge our presence. After one drive-by, the senior agent on the surveillance team told me that immediately after the shootings and Oswald's arrest, Marina had been taken to the home of Irving's police chief, C.J. Wirasnik, for her own protection. Ironically, she watched the coverage of the assassination, her husband's apprehension, and his shooting by Jack Ruby on the police chief's television.

The several nights I spent with the senior agent in a Bureau car observing limited activity at the Paine residence were especially uncomfortable because he insisted on smoking cheap cigars with the windows rolled up (the nights were cold). My clothes reeked of cigar tobacco; several times I almost retched from the smell. On the third night I had had enough, threatening the senior agent by saying that if he lit one more cigar in the Bureau car I would push it right down his throat. Needless to say, he was surprised and irritated to hear this from a first office agent and a rookie at that. When I reported for duty the following evening, I was told that I had been taken off night duty and assigned to the daytime surveillance group. The cigar-smoking senior agent to whom I had been originally assigned avoided me during the remainder of my time in Dallas.

Surveillance during the daytime saw much more activity involving Marina and Ruth Paine. There were visitors to the residence, and, once in a while, the two went shopping at a local market. During one of the shopping trips I got a good look at Marina. Photos I had seen of her—passport and official state identity photographs—depicted her as drab and very plain looking, with a large amount of curly hair pulled back. When I first saw her, she appeared to have cut her hair and was wearing makeup. She was much more attractive in person.

In documenting Marina's daytime contacts, we maintained a log of visitors and the license plates of vehicles that came to the Paine residence. Neither Ruth nor her ex-husband Michael was involved in the assassination in any way. They were completely cooperative with the Bureau, and voluntarily produced all Marina's correspondence and other communications. Ruth Paine was described to me as an avowed Quaker and former college student who was, at the time of the assassination and ensuing surveillance, separated from her husband who nonetheless shared her dislike of Oswald.

After about a week or so my assignment surveilling Marina Oswald ended, and I was sent back to Amarillo. During my absence, considerable work had accumulated, and I put in long hours at the office catching up. The RA was inundated with phone calls from anxious citizens who were eager to transmit all sorts of information—mostly hearsay or speculation—on the assassination. Nonetheless, we diligently recorded this information and followed up on any leads we thought merited further investigation.

My return to the Amarillo RA put me in touch again with my friend and mentor, Tom O'Maley. He was working on a fugitive case and requested my assistance. We apprehended the fugitive in his apartment in Amarillo. During the apprehension something familiar struck my eye. On top of a stack of magazines was a weather-beaten copy of *The FBI Story*. I pointed to the book and asked the fugitive, "What's with this?" To my surprise, he replied, "In order to defeat your enemy you must know him as well as a friend." O'Maley then grabbed the fugitive and said, "Come along *my friend*."

By late 1964, my assignment in Amarillo was nearing its end. One day in early December, I received word from the Dallas office requesting that I get in touch as soon as possible (Tom O'Maley was with me when I received the news). Upon doing so I was told that I had orders to report to the newly established office in Jackson, Mississippi. This was a huge disappointment for me and Jan. We were both hoping to be transferred to the Kansas City office. I hoped to go there because it was active in the field of organized crime and I very much wanted to work in that area. Jan also wanted to go to Kansas City because it was closer to her family home in Colorado. But as an obedient civil servant, I (and Jan) accepted the transfer to Jackson, although with a certain amount of apprehension.

About the time I received word of my new assignment, the Bureau turned over its findings on the Kennedy assassination to the special commission appointed by President Johnson and headed by Chief Justice Earl Warren, commonly known as the Warren Commission. The Commission concluded that Oswald, acting alone, had assassinated President Kennedy. The Commission's report further stated that Oswald had fired from a window of the sixth floor of the Texas School Book Depository building. The report also concluded that there was no prior connection between Oswald and Jack Ruby. The Commission's findings were the result of approximately 25,000 interviews of individuals potentially possessing information relevant to the assassination.

In spite of the FBI's intensive investigation and the Warren Commission's findings, the American public continues to harbor doubts, firmly believing a conspiracy lay behind the assassination. Some of the conspiracy theories are that the Mafia and CIA were behind the murder; that Vice President Johnson, aided by wealthy Texans, perpetrated the crime; and that, based on the number of shots fired and their trajectory, an unidentified person shot the president from behind a grassy knoll. Even former President Johnson, shortly before his death, stated in an interview that he never believed that Oswald had acted alone. Johnson was angered by the CIA's attempts on the life of Cuban dictator Fidel Castro and thought President Kennedy had been killed in retaliation. Although every FBI agent actually involved in the investigation agreed, so far as I am aware, with the Warren Commission's findings and that all of the conspiracy theories have been debunked, many continue to believe them. In fact, public opinion polls show that two-thirds of Americans surveyed do not accept the conclusions of the Warren Commission. This is not surprising in light of all that has been written and said over the decades by those spreading doubts about Oswald's guilt. Moreover, the sheer volume of interviews during the investigation resulted in many inconsistencies—inconsistences seized upon by authors who wove all sorts of conspiracy theories, giving rise to a lucrative cottage industry.

I'm often asked why President Kennedy was shot, especially when I tell the questioner that I worked the assassination and was assigned to the Marina Oswald surveillance. I answer by stating that Oswald was a nobody who murdered a somebody and continually tried to impress those around him that he was an intellectual, which he was not. The facts speak for themselves: Lee Harvey Oswald was a confirmed Marxist who fled his homeland in disgust, then demanded that he be allowed to return when he found out that life under communism was far from what he had expected. He was also a man who tyrannized his wife. In short, Oswald was a nobody who believed that shooting the president would make him a somebody.

The FBI's investigation of the Kennedy assassination was an extraordinarily extensive and highly professional effort. Special Agent Robert Gemberling coordinated the Bureau's investigation in Dallas and was responsible for consolidating the more than 2,300 reports the FBI turned over to the Warren Commission. He performed this task admirably and faithfully.

After his retirement, Gemberling became a nationally recognized authority on the assassination because of his especially close association with the investigation. He was a fierce advocate of the no-conspiracy theory, always pointing out that those who believe there was a conspiracy have failed to produce credible and convincing evidence. He repeatedly emphasized that until he saw such evidence he would remain firmly convinced there was no conspiracy and that both Oswald and Ruby acted alone. Each was seeking recognition according to Gemberling.

Over the years since the assassination I made it a point to tell Gemberling how fortunate I felt to have been part of the investigative team. After 1963, my contact with him was largely at FBI conventions and seminars. One of my last contacts with Bob occurred in the summer of 2003 when The Society of Former Special Agents of the FBI was slated to hold its 50th annual meeting in Denver, Colorado. This would be the society's Golden Jubilee, and it would feature nationally prominent speakers from the law enforcement community, the business world, and the political arena. It occurred to me that since the meeting would take place close to the 40th anniversary of the assassination, Gemberling would be an appropriate choice for one of the convention speakers. I contacted him at his residence in Dallas; unfortunately, Bob was being treated for stomach cancer and undergoing chemotherapy and could not travel to Denver. Even though he would not be able to attend the convention, he told me that he would make an effort to prepare some remarks for me to use at the meeting.

In the letter he wrote to me in 2003 containing his recollections,

Bob emphasized his conviction that both Oswald and Ruby acted alone: "It would appear fitting for me to make a few observations and remarks as the 40th anniversary of the JFK assassination approaches. After almost 40 years, there has been no credible evidence indicating others were involved with either Oswald or Ruby." He also noted his belief that had Oswald been in federal custody following his arrest, he would not himself have been assassinated:

> Many questions have been raised concerning Oswald's death at the hands of Jack Ruby while in custody of the Dallas PD. Four presidents of the United States have been assassinated in our history. Presidents Lincoln, Garfield and McKinley were assassinated during a 36-year period (1865-1901). In 1902, after the assassination of President McKinley, the U.S. Secret Service assumed full responsibility for the protection of the President. But it was not until 1917 that Congress enacted a law making it a federal crime to threaten the life of the President. Apparently, Congress did not consider the possibility someone might go beyond a threat and actually kill him. It was not a violation of federal law to kill the President of the United States on November 22, 1963, and Oswald was never in custody of the federal government.

That Oswald had not been in federal custody had haunted Gemberling for 40 years as he followed the mass of erroneous information fed the public, alleging every kind of conspiracy theory imaginable. On November 22, 1963, the absence of a federal law prohibiting the killing of the president resulted in Oswald remaining in the custody of the Dallas Police Department and charged with murder under Texas law. In August 1965, almost two years after the JFK assassination, Congress finally passed legislation making the killing of the president a federal crime and giving the FBI jurisdiction over its enforcement.

Gemberling went on to write that there was no doubt in his mind that had the 1965 law been on the books on Friday, November 22, 1963, with Oswald in the custody of the FBI rather the Dallas Police Department, Jack Ruby would not have been able to get close enough to murder him that Sunday. The Dallas PD's lax security procedures made it possible for Ruby to shoot Oswald.

Bob's letter contained several interesting and little-known points about the assassination and its investigation:

- Marina Oswald received $70,795 in donations from individuals and organizations throughout the country; Mrs. J.D. Tippit, the widow of the Dallas police officer shot to death by Oswald, received $630,000 from the same sources.
- After securing the U. S. attorney general's approval, the FBI conducted a technical surveillance on the Paine residence during the period after the assassination. Although he was not present, Gemberling understood that one of the agents installing the equipment made a misstep in the attic of the house the Bureau had rented to conduct the surveillance and perforated the sheetrock between the rafters. This necessitated some repair work which was performed with such excellence that the damage was never known to the owner.

- On the morning of the assassination, Oswald left his wedding ring in a cup on the dresser of his wife's room at the Paine residence. He also left $170 in his wallet in a drawer in the dresser. He took only $13.87 with him when he embarked on his mission to shoot JFK, an indication that he did not plan to go far after shooting the president.

Bob Gemberling also mentioned in his letter that since the 1990s Marina had been stating publicly that she no longer believed, based on the evidence presented, that Lee had assassinated the president. She had not said why, but Gemberling thought that she had been influenced by the writings of conspiracy theorists.

Gemberling ended his letter by acknowledging the inevitable consequences of his illness (he died in December 2004). He stated that he had no guarantee he would ever meet St. Peter, but he was confident that if he was fortunate enough to do so, his first words to him will be, "There was no conspiracy."

CHAPTER 8

MISSISSIPPI BURNING

In early December 1964, I checked out of the Dallas office, and Jan and I headed in our car to my next assignment, the FBI office in Jackson, Mississippi, which had been established only six months earlier. As we drove east without much enthusiasm, we discussed what had been taking place in Mississippi, especially stories we had heard about the FBI. We knew about the murders of the three civil rights workers the previous June and the recovery of their bodies six weeks later, which attracted nationwide attention. Much of what we heard indicated that the FBI was not very welcome in the state. There were numerous stories of agents resigning rather than serve there, of sand being poured into the gas tanks of Bureau cars, and even of snakes being placed in those cars. In spite of these stories, we tried to convince ourselves of the benefits of the transfer: the cost of living would be less than in Texas, and, as this was a new office, all the agents would be new to the area and in the same situation as we were.

After arriving in Jackson in mid-December, we decided to look the city over before I reported. Much to our liking we found Jackson to be neat and quiet. We briefly took in some of the outlying suburbs and considered them to be more than satisfactory. This short tour led both of us to believe that we could enjoy our assignment there. I reported to Special Agent in Charge (SAC) Roy Moore (a legendary figure in the Bureau), who greeted me and ordered me to report immediately to the Resident Agency in Meridian, Mississippi. He explained that the FBI's "Special" investigation of the murders of the civil rights workers was being run out of the Meridian Resident Agency by Inspector Joseph Sullivan, another legend in the Bureau. Although I was assigned to the Resident Agency, Moore instructed me to report to Sullivan and assist on the "Special" in any way he desired. By way of explanation, "Special" is the term the Bureau applies to investigation of a major case. They were often long and difficult and conducted by a large number of agents assigned solely to that task. Usually, the SAC of the division in which the incident occurred would supervise the investigation. Thus, Gordon Shanklin, the special agent in charge of the Dallas division, supervised the "Kennedy Special." Other Specials might be assigned to an inspector such as Sullivan, who had a Bureau-wide reputation as a troubleshooter. He had been dispatched personally by Hoover to solve the civil rights murders in an investigation the Bureau called the "MIBURN Special."

Although we had looked forward to living in Jackson, I dutifully headed to Meridian, located more than an hour to the east. Our map indicated that Meridian, the county seat of Lauderdale County, had a population of 40,000. Jan and I were both downhearted as we made our way to my new assignment, Jan more than I. She remarked to me that if she did not find Meridian to her liking that I should consider this as my unaccompanied tour because she was going back to Colorado. At the time I was sure she meant what she said, but, as things turned out, she remained steadfast at my side for the entire period of my assignment in Mississippi.

We arrived in Meridian and I reported to Joe Sullivan, the inspector in charge of the Special. My impression was that he was a no-nonsense type who believed in a full work schedule, meaning Monday through Saturday and a half day on Sunday. When I reported, there were twenty-to-twenty-five agents, including the resident agent, working solely on the MIBURN case. Much of their activity involved developing informants. I discovered that the majority of the agents, both on the Special and those assigned to the Resident Agency, were Yankees—born and raised north of the Mason-Dixon Line. Apparently, Dr. Martin Luther King had complained that most of the FBI agents in the Southern offices were native Southerners. The Bureau reacted by sending a large number of Yankee agents to Mississippi, including me. Since many of the agents assigned to the Special were scheduled to be released shortly and return to their respective home offices, Sullivan told me that I would be working both the MIBURN Special and general investigation leads. Coincidentally, Neshoba County, the focal point of the MIBURN case, would also be my principal area of responsibility in the Meridian Resident Agency.

At that time, the Meridian RA was headed by John Proctor and consisted of two other agents, Don Storaker and Roy Burns. My arrival and that of another transfer agent, Dan Bodine, increased the RA's strength to five. Dan and I became inseparable during our time in Mississippi. He was assigned to Kemper County, which was adjacent to Neshoba County on the latter's east side. We became partners and fast friends, not only because of our geographical proximity and similar responsibilities, but also because we enjoyed working together. I always found Dan to be an excellent partner who always offered assistance and would not hesitate to ask me for help when needed. He was a fine man—loyal, knowledgeable, tactful, and with a good sense of humor.

Situated in east central Mississippi, Neshoba County had a population of approximately 51,000. Philadelphia, its county seat, numbered about 6,000. Although the county's population was 80 percent black, voting registration—9,000 whites but only 2,000 blacks—completely reversed that percentage. Neshoba County also contained the Choctaw Indian Reservation. Located in the northeast part of the county, it was the largest native American reservation east of the Mississippi. According to my fellow agents, the Bureau of Indian Affairs staff on the reservation was excellent. They were aided by members of the Mennonite Church who generously tended to the Choctaws' many needs.

Several factors added to the normal apprehension I would have felt when embarking on any new assignment. Obviously, I was very aware of the high-profile nature of the MIBURN investigation and knew that local law enforcement in Neshoba (and most law enforcement agencies statewide for that matter) would not cooperate with the FBI. Also, I feared that the presence of the Choctaw Reservation would result in a complex intermingling of the problems of African-Americans and native Americans. Indeed, Proctor told me that an Indian from the reservation had first reported the location of the burned vehicle of the civil rights workers.

Before we went to work on the MIBURN case, Proctor suggested that Dan and I find housing for our families, and pointed out areas of the city most likely to be receptive to FBI agents. Jan and I quickly discovered a newly built apartment complex located in the northern part of Meridian. Called The Heritage, it was a gated apartment community with access to a nearby shopping center. Its residents included several influential citizens of Meridian, Navy and Marine Corps officers assigned to the Meridian Naval Air Station, and several FBI agents, some accompanied by their wives.

Segregated drinking fountains (Courtesy, National Archives and Records Administration)

After Jan and I were settled in our apartment we immediately observed the extreme segregation, very much alien to either of us that existed outside our gated community. We were appalled at the prevalence of signs on businesses or public facilities that proclaimed "Whites Only" or "Colored Entrance," and of the separate services for whites and blacks. One of Jan's lasting impressions of the profound impact of such blatant segregation occurred in the context of the birth of our son which took place several months after we arrived. To assist her, we hired a black woman. In spite of Jan's insistence to the contrary, she would not sit at the same table with Jan for lunch or coffee. When Jan took her home, she adamantly refused to sit in the front seat, explaining that it was not right do so. At least in practice, she had accepted white society's demands that blacks "stay in their place," call all white men "Mister," and accept segregated facilities. For any black to challenge these behavioral "norms" or to register to vote would brand him or her an "agitator." Although we found the people in our apartment complex to be friendly and hospitable, we were received very differently outside its bounds. Once we were identified as Yankees we were treated coldly, but not indifferently since the Mississippians always wanted to know what we were doing in their state. When they learned I was with the FBI, they even became confrontational, asking why the Justice Department through the FBI was increasing federal pressure on their fair state.

But the cool attitude we experienced from many ordinary Mississippians during the years we spent in Meridian was insignificant compared to the threats we and the other agents and their families received from the Klan. We were harassed continually, usually by threatening phone calls received at work and at home. For example, an anonymous caller would state that one of our wives had been in an accident and then hang up. Initially, we found the calls to be very disturbing, but they occurred with such frequency that we began to ignore them. In time, they became more of a nuisance than a worry.

When Dan and I reported to the Meridian RA in mid-December 1964, the perpetrators of the murder of the three civil right workers had already been arrested and indicted. For this reason, we felt at first that we had come too late and that the key events had passed us by. But, as we would discover, there was much yet to take place with respect to the case. Moreover, our presence at the center of the investigation and the exciting atmosphere surrounding it dispelled that feeling.

Since both Dan and I were new to the MIBURN case, we had to become familiar with it as soon as possible. Briefings by John Proctor and agents assigned to the Special along with the information contained in the Bureau's files brought us up to speed not only on the status of the investigation but also on the events that had led to the murders.

Ruins of Mt. Zion United Methodist Church, near
Philadelphia, Mississippi, burned June 16, 1964.

The confrontation that resulted in the deaths of the three men on the night of June 21-22, 1964 originated in Neshoba County. Earlier that month the Neshoba Ku Klux Klan had burned the Mt. Zion United Methodist Church, located about eight miles east of Philadelphia. This was one of the first church burnings to take place in the state—forty more would follow. In response to the burning of the church, the three civil rights workers, driving a 1963 Ford station wagon, traveled from Meridian to the Mt. Zion neighborhood:

FBI flyer on three missing civil rights workers.
(Author's personal collection)

Michael Schwerner, age twenty-four, a white Jewish New Yorker had been living in Meridian with his wife, Rita, for about six months. He was the head of the local Council of Federated Organizations (COFO), the coalition of major civil rights organizations coordinating the voter registration drive in Mississippi. Schwerner was despised by the Klan, labeled a "nigger-lovin Jew," and nicknamed "Goatee" for his facial hair. The Klan made it known that Goatee had to be eliminated (killed).

James Chaney, age twenty-one, was an African-American who worked as a plasterer in Meridian. He had been working with Schwerner for several months. He was native to the area and Schwerner used him as a driver and contact with the black community.

Andrew Goodman, age twenty, also a white Jewish New Yorker had arrived in Meridian the day before. He was a student at Queens College and was among the first group of about 1,000 COFO volunteers.

After speaking with people in the Mt. Zion neighborhood, the three men were returning to Meridian by way of the small town of Philadelphia. They were pulled over for speeding within the town limits and confronted by Neshoba County Deputy Sheriff Cecil Price who arrested all three—Chaney for speeding and the other two for investigation. They were incarcerated for about six hours before being released. Chaney paid a $20 fine for speeding, and Price escorted the three to the edge of town. They were last seen headed for Meridian, but never arrived.

When they did not return that evening as expected, the Meridian COFO office contacted the Justice Department's Civil Rights Division and the local FBI. Proctor, the Meridian senior resident agent, quickly reconstructed the details of the three men's arrest and incarceration. He also initially reported that local and state authorities were not making any effort to find them. In fact, many of the local residents believed that the story about three missing men was simply a hoax to get the FBI into their state. Some of the locals felt they would turn up when they realized their hoax had not had the desired effect. Mississippi's governor, Paul Johnson, said that for all he knew the three civil rights workers were in Cuba. In contrast to these flippant comments, almost overnight the nation's attention turned on the little town of Philadelphia and the missing men. The ensuing clamor forced President Johnson and Attorney General Robert F. Kennedy to move on the case. At this point, the Justice Department notified the FBI that the disappearance was to be treated as a kidnapping. Director Hoover immediately dispatched a squad of agents to Meridian to assist the RA in trying to pick up the civil rights workers' trail. This would be the first wave of a force of 150 agents who would participate in what became a mammoth search effort.

Several days after the disappearance of the trio, a Choctaw from the reservation in Neshoba County reported seeing a fire-blackened station wagon, still smoldering, in the Bogue Chitto swamp located in the northeast part of the county. The FBI quickly determined that the vehicle belonged to the civil rights workers. Agents on the scene searched the vehicle and the immediate area, but found no bodies.

The news of the discovery of the car was relayed to Hoover who, in turn, notified President Johnson. Hoover then set up the Special and sent 100 agents into Mississippi to expand the search in the Bogue Chitto swamp where the vehicle was found. He then dispatched his longtime aide, Alex Rosen, who at the time was assistant director for the general investigative division at FBI head-quarters. He would take charge of the search and be assisted by Inspector Sullivan. After Rosen returned to Washington, Sullivan resumed directing the search effort and reported daily to Hoover.

The expanded search continued from dawn to dusk in an area of murky waters, tangled vines, leeches, poisonous snakes, mosquitoes, and chiggers. The agents and some local and state law enforcement officials were joined by a contingent of 400 sailors and a helicopter from the nearby Meridian Naval Air Station. In addition to the difficult terrain and the pests that inhabited it, heat and thunderstorms plagued the searchers. But the intensive and large-scale effort failed to produce any evidence of the missing trio. Hundreds were interviewed but said either that they knew nothing of the missing trio or lied about what they did know. The national media following the search repeatedly reported sightings of the men that turned out to be false.

The White House received regular status briefings. When President Johnson was first informed of the recovery of the civil rights workers' vehicle, he contacted his former Senate colleagues from Mississippi, James Eastland and John Stennis. They both told Johnson that the entire incident was a hoax and that there was no organization in the state capable of doing such a thing. But the president felt otherwise and sent Allen Dulles, the director of the CIA, to confer with Governor Johnson and to assess and evaluate the situation. Dulles concluded that the atmosphere was explosive, and action had to be taken to control the Klan. He also recommended that federal law enforcement presence in the state be increased. As the situation in the state continued to heat up, the president contemplated either activating the National Guard or sending federal troops to Mississippi.

But, as an alternative to deploying troops, Hoover suggested that the FBI open an office in Jackson (then headed by Roy Moore as previously noted) and staff it with 150 agents (over 100 agents were already in the state working on the disappearance of the trio). The president agreed to the suggestion but stipulated that Hoover personally open the office and meet with Governor Johnson to initiate a federal and state effort against the Klan. The president instructed Hoover to put his agents on the Klan, study it intensively, and develop an intelligence system to check on its activities. As a result, the FBI initiated its Anti-Klan Campaign.

CHAPTER 9

THE MIBURN INVESTIGATION

The search for the three missing civil rights workers continued for more than forty days with no success. Inspector Sullivan developed a source who told him the bodies of the men were buried in a recently constructed earthen dam located about five miles southwest of Philadelphia. (It was rumored that the Bureau paid as much as $30,000 for this information.) The property was owned by Olen Burrage and was known as the Old Jolly Place. The inspector then got a search warrant, served it, and brought in a dragline and bulldozer from the Jackson area. After digging down about fifteen feet into the dam, the bodies were found—stacked one on top of the other—forty-four days after their disappearance. The remains were exhumed and taken to the University of Mississippi Medical School in Jackson. Autopsies revealed that all three had been shot at close range with a .38 caliber weapon. Schwerner had one bullet in his lungs, Goodman one in his chest, and Chaney's body three bullets—one in the head and two entering from the back.

The media referred to the source who divulged the location of the bodies as "Mr. X." The source was known only to Inspector Sullivan, and he never publicly revealed his identity. (It's likely that Hoover and others at FBI headquarters probably knew who the source was, given the previously mentioned large amount said to have been paid for the information.) The agents on the Special told Dan and me that some Neshobans had said, "It's not fair—the FBI pays for its information." The agents also said that the payoff generated a lot of suspicion in Philadelphia; everyone was watching to see if a neighbor bought a new car or made a major purchase.

After the recovery of the bodies, the agents assigned to the MIBURN case concentrated on three objectives: identifying the perpetrators; infiltrating the Klan with additional informants; and checking on Klan activities and plans—past, present, and future. To achieve these objectives, the Bureau pressed hard on interviewing and reinterviewing all known and suspected Klansmen in both Lauderdale and Neshoba Counties. In reinterviewing known Klansmen in the Lauderdale County klavern (the Klan's designation for its local units), they discovered that two Klansmen had disappeared from their residences shortly after the bodies were found. Inspector Sullivan thought this to be odd and recognized that, once the two men were located, the Bureau would have a perfect opportunity to conduct an isolation-type interview in which the subjects were questioned separately and away from the crime scene. The two missing Klansmen were identified as Horace Doyle Barnett and James Jordan. Barnett was found in Cullen, Louisiana, and Jordan in Gulfport, Mississippi. Agents interviewed both intensively at those locations and *leaned on* them. (In the Bureau, the term "leaned on" meant constantly contacting and confronting the interview subject wherever that person might be—home, workplace, or social event. We especially used the tactic against uncooperative individuals and made it known to the subject's friends and associates that we were applying pressure. It often produced good results.) Initially both Barnett and Jordan exhibited a defiant attitude, but this was soon broken by the tenacity of the agent interviewers. After many sessions, both admitted membership in the White Knights of the Ku Klux Klan. The agents eventually obtained signed statements from the two which contained details of the triple murder and also identified other individuals who participated directly or assisted in some way. The signed statements differed in that each man claimed he had not participated in the actual shooting. The Bureau closely guarded the statements as Inspector Sullivan and the agents prepared their case against the killers and those who conspired with them. (Senior Resident Agent John Proctor told us that the two agents who obtained the statements were Special Agents James Wooten and Henry Rask. Their efforts constituted a major breakthrough in the MIBURN case.)

As a result of Barnett's and Jordan's statements, Inspector Sullivan obtained arrest warrants; eighteen Klansmen were rounded up, including Neshoba County Sheriff Lawrence Rainey and Deputy Sheriff Cecil Price. They were taken to the Meridian Naval Air Station where they were photographed, fingerprinted, and interviewed. They were then arraigned before U.S. Commissioner Esther Carter. She fixed bond at $5,000 each and ordered them to appear before her in about a week. All made bail and were released.

The news of the arrests made national headlines, and the FBI was praised for its successful efforts. The press noted that the arrests had taken place just short of six months from the time the investigation started. But this praise was short-lived for neither the FBI nor the Justice Department was prepared for the legal roadblocks thrown up by Commissioner Carter. At the hearing she refused to allow into evidence Barnett's and Jordan's signed statements, ruling that they were hearsay. She also ruled that the statements could not be turned over to the defense. The government attorney vehemently objected to her ruling that the statements could not be introduced as evidence, declared that the government would not produce any other evidence in the hearing, and that it intended to request that a grand jury be called as soon as possible. Carter then dismissed the charges against the defendants. Very shortly, Federal District Judge William Harold Cox ordered the grand jury to convene on the case in Jackson.

John Proctor told us, at the time, that the dismissal of the charges seemed to be a victory for the Klan. The defendants were excited and elated by their good fortune. They were all laughing and shaking hands. One was heard to say, "Sheriff Rainey could be elected governor now." However, a huge throng of civil rights workers assembled outside the courthouse, and dismayed by the news of the dismissal, began chanting, "Freedom, freedom, freedom!" The Klan, not to be outdone by the civil rights activists, donned their Klan robes and marched in full regalia in downtown Meridian; they were joined by their fellow Klansmen from the United Klans of America in Tuscaloosa, Alabama.

APPLICATION FOR CITIZENSHIP IN THE INVISIBLE EMPIRE
IN THE

The White Knights
OF THE
Ku Klux Klan
OF
MISSISSIPPI

I, the undersigned, a native born, true and loyal citizen of the United States of America, being a white male Gentile person of temperate habits, sound in mind and a believer in the tenets of the Christian religion, the maintenance of White Supremacy and the principles of a "pure Americanism," do most respectfully apply for membership in the Knights of the Ku Klux Klan through Klarern No._____, Shire of_____.

I guarantee on my honor to conform strictly to all rules and requirements regulating my "naturalization" and the continuance of my membership, and at all times a strict and loyal obedience to your constitutional authority and the constitution and laws of the fraternity, not in conflict with the constitution and constitutional laws of the United States of America and the states thereof. If I prove untrue as a Klansman I will willingly accept as my portion whatever penalty your authority may impose.

The required "klectokon" accompanies this application.

Signed_____ ....Applicant

Endorsed by_____   Residence Address_____

Kl._____   Business Address_____

Kl._____   Date_____, 19_____

The person securing this application must sign on top line above. NOTICE—Check the address to which mail may be sent.

Application for Klan membership. (Author's personal collection)

During the demonstrations by the Klan in Meridian, Dan Bodine and I arrived and became involved in the case. After an extensive period of briefings and study, we were ready to start work. One of our first tasks was to help with the large number of "greenies" that arrived from the Bureau almost daily. "Greenies" (called that because they came on green paper) were allegations of civil rights violations that demanded immediate investigation. Usually, the agent to whom they were assigned had five-to-seven days to complete the investigation. Dan and I handled many of the "greenies" that involved Kemper and Neshoba counties. In addition to the "greenies," our work included routine investigations and other MIBURN-related inquiries. We also assisted the MIBURN group in attempting to develop informants in our assigned areas.

After several months of almost daily trips to Neshoba County I found it hard to develop a friend, much less an informant. Usually, after I entered the county in my readily recognizable Bureau car (it had a large mast antenna affixed to its rear), I would hear three clicks on the Mississippi Highway Patrol radio that was standard equipment in all Bureau cars. The three clicks told anyone with one of those radios that the FBI was in the area. Thus alerted, local law enforcement would be on the lookout to observe whom I might be contacting. On one occasion, when Dan and I were conducting interviews at the COFO office in the black section of Philadelphia, we heard several gunshots and the sound of bullets ricocheting off the cinderblock building. We both hurried to the front entrance, but no one was in sight. We conducted a quick survey of some of the neighboring residents, but none of them saw or heard anything unusual. We could only assume that when the Klan observed our Bureau car in front of the COFO building we became targets for a drive-by shooting. Luckily, no one was injured in the incident.

Another of my duties was to check Neshoba County's voting registration records maintained in the clerk and recorder's office. After explaining to the clerk exactly what I wanted, without a word he would place the registration book on the counter, return to his desk, and ignore me. This routine went on for several years. Not once did the clerk speak to me! Because of my almost daily trips to the Neshoba County courthouse I'm sure I became well known to many of those accused of participating in the murders, including Sheriff Rainey and Deputy Sheriff Price. I had several conversations with Price, primarily dealing with the bombings of the Nanih Waiya Mennonite Church. Constructed by the Mennonites, the church provided assistance to the Choctaw Indians. It was bombed three times, and I told Price that these bombings were not only senseless but also might incite the Choctaws. He never did reply to my observations.

Sheriff Rainey, whom I saw frequently in the courthouse hallway, also ignored me. But, after about a year or so, he surprised me with an acknowledgment. After exchanging brief greetings over a period of time, in August 1966 he agreed to talk to me. He told me that the Bureau was wrong in believing that he was a member of the Klan. Although he admitted that he had attended numerous Klan rallies throughout Mississippi and Alabama, he emphatically denied ever being a Klansman, had never taken the Klan oath, and had never paid dues to any Klan organization. He said repeatedly that his close associations with prominent Klan members were for a law enforcement purpose—to keep on top of what the Klan was doing in Neshoba County. Rainey also told me he did not know anything about the killings; he claimed he was visiting his wife in the hospital in Meridian the night the three civil rights workers disappeared. He did admit that he had returned to Philadelphia to eat supper with his brother-in-law, but then had gone back to Meridian with clothes for his wife. Despite Rainey's denial, we knew without a doubt that he was an active Klansman. I believed that the story about visiting his wife in the hospital the night of the killings was an attempt to establish an alibi—the Grand Jury was then in session in Jackson.

Informants were essential to solving the MIBURN case. Since the Bureau had to contend with a hostile and uncooperative white populace in Mississippi, it had to improvise to get the necessary information. We obtained it by using paid informants. Indeed, the entire MIBURN case was based on information they provided.

Our normal procedure was to conduct interviews with an individual to assess their potential to provide information. If we determined that the person might have useful information and be receptive to our obtaining it, we would appeal to their sense of duty, indicating that they would be performing a patriotic service to their country by assisting us.

After the murders, the Bureau made a major effort to develop informants within the Klan. Two agents who were temporarily assigned to the Special succeeded in getting close to and gaining the confidence of a young Methodist minister, Delmar Dennis, who was a Klan propagandist. The two agents quickly recognized Dennis' potential as an information source, but were both reassigned to their home offices before they could exploit him. At their urging, Inspector Sullivan assigned Dennis to me. Other factors also influenced my selection: I was the agent responsible for Neshoba County, where the case had originated, and Dennis' brother, also a minister, lived in the county.

Delmar Dennis, the twenty-four-year-old minister assigned to me, was well known among segregationists as a prolific writer and pamphleteer espousing Klan causes. Little did I realize at that time that he would be crucial to shattering and destroying the Mississippi Klan. Dennis was clean cut, fairly well educated, and handsome. He also possessed an almost photographic memory and demonstrated extraordinary powers of observation and retention. He easily remembered license plates, phone numbers, and names. Especially significant, he was the trusted aide of Sam Bowers, the Imperial Wizard of the White Knights of the Mississippi Klan.

Despite his great potential as an informant and although he was well paid, Dennis was not easy to exploit. He had a big ego that required continuous stroking. I made him feel important by emphasizing how much the Bureau needed him. I was also able to appeal to his patriotism. At this time the United States was involved in the Vietnam War. Dennis said that he regretted not serving in the military. I pointed out that he could serve his country just as well by cooperating with us. Additionally, I frequently reminded him that as a man of the cloth he could never condone the Klan's violence and the bloodshed that resulted. Apparently, these appeals paid off because Dennis soon became the Bureau's eyes and ears into the Klan's secret inner workings.

Meeting with Dennis presented problems. Meridian, with a population of 40,000, was a fairly small city. Dennis was a well-known church pastor and a popular Klansman. Thus, secure places to meet and debrief him unobserved were extremely limited. Consequently, when his pastoral duties provided justification, we would meet in Jackson or across the state line in Alabama.

The Bureau was eager to obtain information about the Klan. If anything happened involving it, I met with Dennis to obtain information that would help us evaluate what had occurred. After our meetings, I put my notes into reports or memos almost immediately (recorders were not part of an agent's equipment in the 1960s). Often I was writing these memos at the same time I was fielding telephone inquiries from Jackson requesting the information Dennis had just provided.

Meetings with Dennis in and around Meridian were dicey and dangerous. They took place at night and in secluded parks. We would rendezvous at a designated location; usually I used my own car but sometimes a Bureau vehicle. I recall one nocturnal meeting in a state park located on Route 39 in Kemper County. We arrived at the designated site late in the evening in separate vehicles. We sat at one of the picnic tables, and I debriefed Dennis for about an hour. I then returned to my Bureau car and began the return trip to Meridian. I was traveling on a lonely back road when I heard a rattling sound coming from underneath the dashboard. My first thought was that we had been spotted and that the Klan had placed a snake in my unlocked Bureau car while I was debriefing Dennis. I cautiously brought the car to a stop on the side of the road. Then I opened the door and tried to jump out. But I forgot about my seat belt and wound up half outside the car and half still inside secured by the seat belt. My effort to get out of the car while still in my seat belt bruised my midsection and legs. The rattling I had heard turned out to be a large leaf in the heater vent.

After this incident I decided to use the Meridian Naval Air Station located outside the city limits to debrief Dennis. I was on very friendly terms with the Navy intelligence personnel stationed there. Nick Ammons, the head of the unit, was a neighbor and a good friend. He gave me a key to their interview rooms. He asked no questions; he requested only that I make sure all of the lights were turned off whenever I finished. From this point on Dennis and I would enter the base, and I was able to debrief him in a safe and secure area.

After many interviews over an extended period, I felt confident enough in my relationship with Dennis and of his knowledge of Klan activities to ask him to relate the Klan's version of the murders. This was all hearsay information since Dennis was not present when the men were killed. Nonetheless, I felt the information he obtained from Klansmen who were there or who had knowledge of what happened should be made a matter of record.

The following is what Dennis said Klansmen had told him about the murders. The Neshoba Klavern of the White Knights had burned the Mt. Zion United Methodist Church in an effort to lure Schwerner, who had been marked for elimination, into the county.

Schwerner, accompanied by Chaney and Goodman, did exactly as they had hoped. An unknown party notified Deputy Sheriff Price of the trio's presence. Price arrested the three and placed them in the county jail for six hours. This gave him enough time to notify Edgar Ray Killen, a Baptist preacher and the head of the Neshoba Klavern, that Schwerner and two other civil rights workers were in jail. Killen then traveled to Meridian and conferred with the Lauderdale Klavern, which put together an execution squad consisting of Doyle Barnett, who owned a garage in Meridian; James Jordan, a salesman; Wayne Roberts, a bouncer in a local nightclub; Jimmy Arledge and James Snowden, both commercial truck drivers; and Billy Wayne Posey, a service station operator. After meeting with the Lauderdale Klavern, Killen, the architect of the plot, headed back to Philadelphia to establish an alibi. The execution group also traveled to Philadelphia and awaited word from Price as to when the trio was released from the county jail. After receiving this notification, both Price and the execution group followed the three men who were headed toward Meridian. Price, flashing his red lights, pulled the trio's car over. He shoved Chaney into the back seat of their car, and put Schwerner and Goodman into his patrol car. The executioners then drove both cars to a cutoff on the highway. When they stopped, Wayne Roberts rushed to Price's patrol car, pulled Schwerner out, and yelled, "Are you that nigger lover?" Schwerner's last words were, "Sir, I know how you feel." Roberts then shot Schwerner and abruptly turned and shot and killed Goodman who had also been taken out of the vehicle. Jordan then pulled Chaney out of the trio's station wagon, shot him, and yelled, "You didn't leave me anything but a nigger, but at least I killed me a nigger!" Jordan's and Barnett's signed statements were contradictory. Jordan disclaimed any participation in the killings. Barnett claimed that Jordan shot Chaney, but could not remember how many times. FBI ballistic evidence confirmed that Jordan had fired the bullet that entered Chaney's back and lodged in his abdomen and that the weapon that killed Schwerner and Goodman also the fired the fatal shot into Chaney's brain. The executioners then stacked the three bodies in the station wagon. Posey drove the station wagon, followed in another car by the other executioners, to a preselected site, an earthen dam under construction. Herman Tucker, a bulldozer operator, met them at the site. The bodies were removed from the station wagon and dragged to the dam where Tucker buried them with his bulldozer. Tucker then drove the station wagon to the Bogue Chitto swamp, doused it in gasoline, and set it afire.

After the triple murder, the Klansmen who had participated in the killings boasted about what they had done. This is how Dennis found out what had happened that night.

CHAPTER 10

FROM ARRESTS TO TRIAL

On January 11, 1965, Judge Cox convened a federal grand jury which indicted eighteen defendants including Rainey and Price. U.S. marshals made the arrests which were not accompanied by demonstrations or fanfare. Sixteen defendants reappeared before U.S. Commissioner Carter and all were released on $5,750 bond each. James Jordan voluntarily surrendered to the FBI in Atlanta. Horace Doyle Barnett was arrested in Shreveport and released on $5,000 bond.

Almost two more years would pass between the arrests and the start of the MIBURN trial. The delay resulted from numerous legal complications. These included the initial dismissal of the complaint by U.S. Commissioner Carter, an unexpected setback for the government case. In her ruling, Carter declared that the signed statements obtained by Bureau agents from Horace Doyle Barnett and James Jordan were hearsay since neither had been present at the hearing. Further legal complications ensued after the grand jury indictments. Judge Cox had ruled that the accused men could only be tried on misdemeanor charges and that the government had no jurisdiction in the matter. However, the Supreme Court overturned this ruling stating that all the defendants should be charged with a felony—conspiring to deprive the three civil rights workers of their rights. To add to the delay, the defense charged that the indicting grand jury had been illegally drawn. The Department of Justice agreed and the indictments were thrown out, freeing the defendants from all charges. But in February 1967, a legally drawn grand jury in Jackson reinstated the conspiracy indictments against the original defendants. There were three exceptions: Jimmy Lee Townsend was not reindicted and the names of Ethel Glen (Hop) Barnette, the Democratic Party nominee for Neshoba County sheriff, and Sam Bowers, the Imperial Wizard, were added to the list of indicted conspirators.

During the long period before the trial began, the Meridian RA essentially became a field office for Assistant Attorney General for Civil Rights John Doar and several of his staff attorneys. Doar asked me to accompany him in and around Meridian and Philadelphia as he contacted known civil rights activists. He told them to contact me if they had any complaints. In addition to responding to these civil rights complaints, I also continued to work Delmar Dennis and other informants (my responsibilities in this area were now statewide), and, of course, to handle the "greenies" coming from the Bureau that involved Neshoba County.

Although there was limited Klan activity in the Meridian-Philadelphia area, the Klan was very active in other parts of the state. When incidents occurred, I contacted Dennis to determine if he had any information. A typical example of the assistance he provided took place in early January 1966 when the house of a prominent black citizen in Hattiesburg, Mississippi, was bombed, killing the owner, Vernon Dahmer. Sam Bowers had organized and directed the bombing. At my request, the day after the bombing Dennis met with Bowers who admitted his role in the incident. We immediately forwarded this information to the Jackson office. Thanks to Dennis, the Bureau had its first lead on the case within forty-eight hours and resulted in the arrest and convictions of several Klansmen, including Bowers.

My duties in the Meridian RA went beyond civil rights matters; they included general investigative work. The events in Mississippi took place during the Vietnam War and some of our investigations were associated with that conflict. For example, I recall looking for an Army deserter in and around Philadelphia. I subsequently found out that his family had moved to a rural location near Carthage, Mississippi, about halfway between Meridian and Jackson and north of both. After a long trip on dirt roads I located the family. I explained the situation to his father, but he was not cooperative. I told him that his son was considered to be a fugitive; if he did not return to military control, he would be fair game for any law enforcement agency. The father pondered this and finally told me his son was working at the Pan-Am gas station in Jackson. I immediately contacted the Jackson office on my Bureau radio, gave them the information, asked them to pick the deserter up. The father was amazed at how quickly I had transmitted the information and expressed disbelief that I had actually talked to faraway Jackson via the radio in my Bureau car. I explained to him that the FBI was the world's premier law enforcement agency and that it possessed the most up-to-date electronic equipment and employed the most advanced law enforcement techniques. We parted amiably, but the father continued to express doubt about the Bureau's communications capabilities. I then attempted to start my vehicle, but the combination of the lengthy radio transmission to Jackson and my demonstrations for the father's benefit had apparently run my battery down. I had no other recourse but to ask his assistance. He agreed, and hitching up his mules to my car, pulled it with me inside several miles on the lousy back roads to the nearest gas station. As I sat in the Bureau car looking at the back ends of the two mules, I couldn't help but think what a boob I was. I had been extolling the FBI as the leading law enforcement agency in the world, only to have to resort to being transported by two mules!

As I indicated earlier, my responsibilities in Neshoba County also included the Choctaw Indian Reservation. For the most part, the Choctaws remained aloof during the civil rights turmoil of the 1960s. Nonetheless, they suffered the same racism and segregation as black Mississippians. For example, they were required to sit in the sections reserved for blacks in movie theaters and restaurants, and were required to send their children to the black schools (actually, most did not send them to school at all). In a departure from their usual aloofness, a group of Choctaws were outraged that the Neshoba Klan had burned and bombed their church, the Nanih Waiya Mennonite Church, three different times. As I mentioned before, I had spoken with Deputy Sheriff Price and told him that the Choctaws were likely to go on the warpath in response to these senseless acts. I also conferred with agents of the Bureau of Indian Affairs and passed on some pertinent information regarding the Neshoba Klavern. I told them that the Neshoba Klan would be holding a rally in the northern part of the county in an effort to raise funds for the White Christian Legal Defense Fund, a Klan-sponsored activity. On the night of the rally the Choctaws dressed up in full war paint and broke it up. They shouted, screamed, and brandished hammers, axes, and tire irons, terrifying the white-sheeted Klansmen who raced to their cars, holding the hems of their white sheets in their hands so they would not trip over them as they tried to escape. My partner Dan and I never saw anything quite as funny as grown men running in terror so daintily. I was flattered that my boss, Roy Moore, was pleased how I had handled the situation. In later speeches to civic groups, he described what happened: "You should have seen them running with their skirts up!"

During the investigation of the murder of Vernon Dahmer, the black civil rights worker, in Hattiesburg in January 1966, the FBI brought a large number of agents to the city to assist in arresting the Klansmen involved. Included among them were several first office agents who were unfamiliar with Roy Moore's dynamic manner and bulldog determination. He was a fiery and inspirational leader who insisted on precise adherence to any plan that he proposed—in this case, the arrest plan. Moore spoke to the agents in a large meeting room of a local motel very early in the morning (the arrests were to begin at 5:00 a.m.). We were divided into teams; each team was assigned a specific subject to arrest. All of us were armed, some with shotguns. We eagerly awaited for Moore to describe the arrest plan. We were not disappointed. It was thorough and detailed, emphasizing the need for close coordination. He concluded his presentation with some fiery comments: "Now get out there and do your duty! Show them we're mad as hell, and we're not going to put up with these kluckers! Remember, the whole country is watching—NOW GO!" After this inspiring sendoff, we all stood up and shouted:

"Let's get them!" In the excitement, a young first office agent carrying a 12-gauge shotgun discharged a round into the ceiling. Debris fell from above. After a painful silence, one of the team leaders remarked: "Can anyone use an extra shotgun?" But in spite of this mishap the arrests went off as planned.

Ironically, Dahmer's killing was the last big civil rights murder in Mississippi. It was also a turning point for the Magnolia state, for with FBI-produced evidence (which Delmar Dennis provided) the state of Mississippi, for the first time, gave four white men life sentences for a civil rights murder.

At one point during my assignment in Meridian, I presented a counter-intelligence proposal to Roy Moore. It consisted of forming a group to be called the Patrick Henry Society made up of disappointed and disillusioned Klansmen. I felt that such an organization would give these men a new identity and, with the help of Delmar Dennis who would lead the group, enable us to contain them. I submitted a memo outlining the proposal to Moore, but he turned it down. We discussed the plan at length; he wanted to adhere to the tactic of divide and conquer—the more direct head-on approach. Moore was right. The Bureau's successes against the Klan in Mississippi testify to that. (He kiddingly accused me of trying to incorporate CIA tactics into the anti-Klan operation!)

CHAPTER 11

THE MIBURN TRIAL

On October 9, 1967, just over three years and three months after the murders of James Chaney, Andrew Goodman, and Michael Schwerner, Imperial Wizard Sam Bowers and seventeen other members of the White Knights of the Ku Klux Klan of Mississippi (WKKKKOM) went to trial in federal court in Meridian. It would last less than two weeks. I was present for some of the sessions; Jan attended all of them.

All eighteen Klansmen went to trial, not for murdering the three men, but for conspiring to obstruct their civil rights. The maximum penalty for this charge was ten years' imprisonment and a $5,000 fine. The defendants were:

1. Bernard Akin, a Meridian mobile home dealer.
2. Jimmy Arledge, a Meridian truck driver.
3. Ethel Glen (Hop) Barnette, the Democratic nominee for Neshoba County sheriff.
4. Horace Doyle Barnett, a Meridian salesman, who gave

a signed statement but then turned mute before and after the MIBURN trial.

5. Travis Barnett, a mechanic and half-brother of Doyle.
6. Sam Bowers, Jr., Imperial Wizard of the WKKKKOM.
7. Olen Burrage, on whose farm the bodies of the three slain men were found.
8. James (Pete) Harris, a Meridian truck driver.
9. Frank Herndon, operator of a Meridian drive-in restaurant.
10. Reverend Edgar Ray Killen, leader of the Neshoba Klan.
11. Billy Wayne Posey, a service station operator from Williamsville, Mississippi.
12. Deputy Sheriff Cecil Price of Neshoba County.
13. Sheriff Lawrence Rainey of Neshoba County.
14. Wayne Roberts, a Meridian nightclub bouncer.
15. Jerry Sharpe, who ran a pulpwood supply house.
16. Jimmy Snowden, a Meridian laundry truck driver.
17. Herman Tucker, who built the dam in which the trio were buried.
18. Richard Willis, a Philadelphia police officer and the last to see the three men alive.

Federal District Judge Cox, a native Mississippian, presided over the trial. Many believed him to be pro-Klan (he once referred to a group of black voter registration applicants as "a bunch of chimpanzees"). But the notion that Cox would be biased was quickly dispelled; on the first day of the trial he forcefully admonished the defense, indicating that he was not going to allow a farce to be made of the proceedings. John Doar, assistant attorney general for civil rights, led the prosecution team. Attorneys from the Neshoba Bar Association represented most of the defendants. The jury was selected quickly and without incident; it consisted of seven women and five men, all white.

After the preliminaries were out of the way, Doar outlined the government's case. He was quite candid about the methods the government had employed: "This was a very intensive investigation by the FBI. It paid for information leading to the solution, and witnesses will testify here who have been paid for information they have furnished." He then told the story of the arrest of the three civil rights workers, their release and subsequent interception by Klansmen, and their murders.

The first prosecution witness, one of the Bureau's informants, was Sergeant Wallace Miller of the Meridian Police Department. He identified Akin, Arledge, Doyle Barnett, Travis Barnett, Bowers, Harris, Herndon, Killen, Roberts, and Snowden as Klansmen. He also testified that the Klan had planned to eliminate Schwerner and that one of the defendants had told him that the three men had been killed and buried in a dam.

More than a dozen witnesses followed Miller to the stand. They testified to the identities of the three victims, identified the bullets that killed them, and discussed other technical points.

The second day of the trial was Delmar Dennis' day in court. His appearance was a surprise. None of the defendants knew that Dennis, a fellow Klansman and trusted aide of Sam Bowers, had been an FBI informant for over three years. In fact, several weeks prior to the trial Bowers had said, "There's only one man I trust in the state, that's Delmar Dennis." Imagine his shock as he watched Dennis enter the courtroom and take the witness stand.

Calmly and deliberately Dennis testified to the following :

1. He admitted that he was a member of the Klan; in fact, he had been sworn in by Edgar Ray (Preacher) Killen, the leader of the Neshoba Klan.

2. He said that he had served as the Mississippi Klan's Chaplain and Province Titan, and in the latter role had been a courier between Bowers and the Lauderdale Klavern and had delivered funds from Bowers to individual Klansmen.

3. He identified several of the defendants as Klan members, including Sheriff Rainey and Deputy Sheriff Price.

4. He corroborated previous testimony regarding the Klan, including its intention to kill Schwerner.

5. He told of intimate conversations he had with Bowers, who said that he was pleased with the slaying of Michael Schwerner because it was the first time Christians had executed a Jew.

Dennis' powerful and detailed testimony shattered the invisible empire of Sam Bowers and the WKKKKOM.

For its part, the defense attacked the prosecution witnesses, but without directly challenging the truth of their testimony. The defense's main contention was that the prosecution witnesses should not be believed because they were paid FBI informants. In an attempt to discredit Dennis' testimony, the defense put his ex-wife on the stand. After closing arguments by the defense, Judge Cox turned the case over to the jury.

Author and informant Delmar Dennis (right)
leaving courthouse in Meridian, Mississippi,
after Dennis' testimony. (Courtesy, Corbis Images)

The jury deliberated for two days. During this period, they sent several notes to Judge Cox requesting further instructions on certain terms used in the trial. A final note reported that they were hopelessly deadlocked. Upon hearing this, Judge Cox ordered the jury back into the courtroom. He gave them the famous "Allen Charge." (Named after the 1896 Supreme Court case, Allen v. the United States, and also known as the "dynamite charge," it consists of instructions given by the judge to encourage juries that are deadlocked to reach a verdict.) Judge Cox told the jurors not to surrender their honest convictions simply for the sake of returning a verdict, but that they should consult with one another and not hesitate to change their opinions. He reemphasized that each defendant stood on his own; the verdict did not have to be the same for all of the defendants. He closed by saying that he had received more communications from this jury than any since he had been on the bench, but he attributed the many notes to the large number of defendants in the case.

The "dynamite charge" prompted a remark by Wayne Roberts to Deputy Sheriff Price that, "We know where we can get some dynamite to speed up a decision." A U.S. marshal heard the comment and reported it to the judge.

On the morning of October 20, 1967, history was made in Mississippi. Seven white men were convicted of conspiracy to obstruct civil rights. The jury acquitted eight of the defendants, but was unable to reach a verdict in the case of three. Convicted were Jimmy Arledge, Doyle Barnett, Sam Bowers, Billy Wayne Posey, Cecil Price, Wayne Roberts, and Jimmy Snowden. Akin, Travis Barnett, Burrage, Harris, Herndon, Rainey, Tucker, and Willis were acquitted and released as were the three men who received no verdict—E.G. ("Hop") Barnette, Sharpe, and "Preacher" Killen. A female juror stated that she could never convict a minister. (The Justice Department dropped the charges against Barnette, Killen, and Sharp, but almost forty years later the State of Mississippi retried Killen who was convicted of three counts of manslaughter and sentenced to twenty years for each count.)

The seven convicted defendants were to be released on bond with the exception of Cecil Price and Wayne Roberts. Both appeared before Judge Cox who, surprisingly, denied them bond. He related that he was aware of the dynamite threat and wanted both men jailed over the weekend. Then speaking directly to the duo, he admonished them severely saying: "If you think you can intimidate this court you are just as badly mistaken as you possibly can be. I'm not going to let any wild man loose on any civilized society. I want you locked up." A few days later, Judge Cox called Bowers, Price, and Roberts before the bench. He told them that he knew of a report that dynamite had been stolen from a Meridian dealer on the day the trial opened. He continued that he was going to release them on bond pending their appeals. But if any dynamite was used in any sort of violence in the Southern District of Mississippi, he threatened, their bonds would be cancelled: "I just don't want anymore of this strong-arm stuff."

On December 29, 1967, Judge Cox sentenced Sam Bowers and Wayne Roberts to the maximum prison term provided under federal law for conspiracy—each received a ten-year sentence. Cecil Price and Billy Wayne Posey received six-year sentences; Arledge, Doyle Barnett, and Snowden, three years each. Collectively, the convicted men began to be referred to as the "Neshoba Seven."

Although many misguided citizens in Mississippi regretted the outcome of the trial, they had no idea how much time, effort, and money had been expended to overcome the forces of unreason and brutality. Their anger focused on Delmar Dennis. He was called a Judas, a traitor to the white race, and a shameful disgrace. He was shot at several times at his home and in his car. Klan sympathizers also attempted unsuccessfully to have him arrested and charged with assault with intent to kill, and other offenses.

Author paying Delmar Dennis (left) for services rendered to the FBI. (Author's personal collection)

I began to realize that Dennis had to be relocated so he could begin a new life elsewhere. After much discussion with Bureau officials and with his consent, he was relocated to Santa Fe, New Mexico. The Bureau compensated him generously for the move. However, he stayed in Santa Fe for only a short time and made numerous trips to Los Angeles where he appeared on the Joe Pyne radio show. Pyne was a controversial, generally conservative radio and television talk show host with contacts in the John Birch Society, a radical right-wing political organization that was ardently anti-communist and advocated limited government. Consequently, Dennis came under the influence of the society, eventually moved to Los Angeles, and became one of its spokesmen, particularly on Klan matters.

My contacts with Dennis were very limited after his departure from Santa Fe. A short note or Christmas card was the extent of our correspondence, but I will never forget the dramatic and exciting experiences I shared with him.

Although the convictions of Sam Bowers and his Klansmen were a staggering blow to the WKKKKOM, it did not bring an immediate end to violence in the state. For several months the Americans for the Preservation of the White Race, a splinter group of the White Knights, launched hit-and-run night attacks on black homes and churches throughout Mississippi, and added a new target of their hatred—Jews. In 1967, they bombed the new synagogue and the home of Rabbi Perry Nussbaum in Jackson, and, in 1968, dynamited the synagogue in Meridian. In response, the Jewish community established a fund that the Meridian Police Department, guided by the FBI, used to pay informants who revealed that the Klan planned to bomb the home of Meyer Davidson, a businessman and leader in the Meridian Jewish community. Thus informed, the Meridian police and the FBI set a trap. They held daily strategy sessions, made plans to evacuate the Davidson family, and set up a stakeout of their home. All potential escape routes would be covered. My partner, Dan Bodine, and I were assigned to one of these. A demolition team from the Meridian Naval Air Station would be on call.

Initially, the Meridian police believed Thomas Albert Tarrants III and Joe Danny Hawkins, the two top Klan "hit men," would attempt the bombing. But, at the last moment, Kathy Ainsworth, a school teacher and Tarrants' companion, took Hawkins' place. Shortly after midnight on June 30, 1968, the two bombers walked across the lawn of the Davidson home with twenty-nine sticks of dynamite which would be ignited by a mercury fuse. A gun battle erupted. Joseph (Mike) Hatcher, a Meridian police officer, and an innocent bystander were wounded in the shooting. Ainsworth was killed and Tarrants apprehended.

This episode signaled the end of Klan activity in Mississippi. When I arrived in late 1964, the Klan numbered about 5,000 and their murders, bombings, beatings, and other terrorist acts had escalated to about 250 per year. At the time of the gun battle in Meridian three-and-a-half years later, Klan strength was estimated at less than 500, with only 50 members considered to be "hardcore." The relentless pressure applied by the FBI and local law enforcement, supported by the state's decent citizens, to hold the Klan responsible for its acts had caused the reduction. This hooded society of bigots, who usually struck at night, could not take the heat.

CHAPTER 12

RETURN TO COLORADO: THE DENVER OFFICE

After the Neshoba Seven's successful prosecution and Delmar Dennis' relocation, I looked forward to a long-promised transfer to Colorado, where Jan and I wanted to live. Roy Moore, the SAC in Jackson, assured me that if I "stayed the course" until the MIBURN case was resolved, he would ensure my transfer to the FBI's Denver office.

Ironically, shortly after the MIBURN trial concluded I was scheduled to attend a Bureau in-service firearms training course in Washington, D.C. Moore contacted me and said that I should see Director Hoover and personally request a transfer to Denver. I adamantly refused because the word within the Bureau was that he did not favor baldheaded agents and I did not want to press my luck with him. However, while attending the training I was surprised when I was called to Hoover's office. Moore, unknown to me, had arranged for me to meet with the director. Needless to say, on my way to his office, I was not just apprehensive but downright frightened and upset. Mr. Hoover's influential and well-known secretary, Helen Gandy ushered me into his office. I was in awe. I had previously met the director and had shaken his hand when I completed my agent training years earlier, but this was nothing like that occasion. Hoover extended his hand (which I very cautiously grasped) and addressed me by name. When he sat down behind his desk, I sat in one of the chairs directly in front of it. After exchanging pleasantries about Roy Moore, Hoover turned to the many obstacles the Bureau had faced in Mississippi. In his view, the civil rights organizations were one of these, and he expressed disdain for them. My response to this unexpected tirade consisted of "yes sir" and "no sir." After his vigorous criticism of the civil rights groups, Hoover abruptly stood up. I had sensed some activity behind me, but was afraid to look away from him. Suddenly, out of the blue, Hoover said that when an opening occurred in the Denver office I would be considered for a transfer. Until that moment, my next assignment had not come up in our conversation. Our meeting was over. It seemed surreal. I'm not sure how I found my way back to the in-service training location. I was in a complete daze, although I think I did remember to thank Hoover.

Not long after this, in May 1969, Jan and I found ourselves on the way to Denver—the office that I had listed as my preferred assignment. Even though we were elated at having finally achieved our goal, we were both sad to have to say goodbye to our many Mississippi friends. Jan cried as much on our departure as she had when we first entered the Magnolia state. The friends we left behind were kind and gracious and always willing to share their deepest feelings with us. We were flattered that they chose to confide in us in this way. We had talked with them about the changes that would take place in Mississippi in the years to come. Although recognizing that changes would inevitably occur, they also believed that racial divisions would always exist. After we left Mississippi, we corresponded frequently with our friends, and many of them have visited us in "Yankee Land" over the years.

OFFICE OF THE DIRECTOR

UNITED STATES DEPARTMENT OF JUSTICE

FEDERAL BUREAU OF INVESTIGATION

WASHINGTON, D.C. 20535

June 10, 1965

PERSONAL

Mr. Donald J. Cesare
Federal Bureau of Investigation
Jackson, Mississippi

Dear Mr. Cesare:

Your exceptionally fine performance relative to the developing and handling of a confidential source of information of much value to the Bureau is most noteworthy and I do not want the occasion to pass without commending you.

Through the skillful manner in which this source was interviewed, you and a fellow agent were able to gain his cooperation, thereby obtaining information which had previously been inaccessible. I am aware of the numerous problems you encountered and I want you to know I appreciate your efficient work in this important field.

Sincerely yours,

J. Edgar Hoover

J. Edgar Hoover commends author for his work in Mississippi. (Author's personal collection)

My arrival in Denver was a bit odd as there had been few transfers to that office over the years. Most of us knew that the FBI hierarchy did not consider Denver to be one of the top assignments among the Bureau's fifty-nine field offices. Thirty-seven special agents were assigned to its headquarters in the city and twenty-five special agents stationed in the resident agencies throughout Colorado and Wyoming, its area of responsibility. The agents in Denver were old timers who had been there for many years; they were all determined to reach the mandatory retirement age of fifty-five while assigned to that office.

Within the Denver office was a palace guard composed of agents, usually old timers, who were close both professionally and socially to Scott Werner, the special agent in charge. These agents were usually chosen to handle the most important cases. I vividly recall a civil rights incident that took place shortly after my arrival. In Denver at that time, students were being bused to attend schools out of their neighborhoods to correct racial imbalances. In retaliation, unknown parties were burning school buses. Werner quickly dispatched members of the palace guard to investigate. Someone remembered that I had just reported in from Mississippi; he told Werner that this was exactly the type of work I had been doing. Werner's comment was "He doesn't have enough stripes," meaning that I was not seasoned enough in the division to handle this type of case. I wasn't offended. After years of handling civil rights cases in Mississippi and the crushing workload in the Jackson office of more than 2,000 cases a month, I was more than eager for a respite and change from that kind of work.

As the new guy in the office, I was assigned to the organized crime squad headed by a senior agent with two other agents who performed most of the field work. As the new member I was given a few old cases which I called "old dogs" because they had been open for a long time and required little management. They mainly involved longtime gamblers with suspected organized crime connections. Interspersed with these cases I occasionally assisted in investigating bank robberies and in apprehending military deserters and other fugitives. I especially remember helping an older agent with a fugitive case. He arrested the fugitive without incident and wanted to give me the experience of booking the individual into the city jail. I took the handcuffed fugitive to the jail complex and rapped loudly on the door. Soon a jailer lifted a peek latch. I said quite forcefully, holding out my credentials for him to see, that I was Don Cesare with the FBI and that I had a prisoner. The jailer unlocked the door and caustically commented (referring to me), "You look like *you* belong in here!" This didn't sit well with me, and I found myself beginning to dislike my Denver headquarters assignment.

To add to my dissatisfaction I found the work assigned to me to be unchallenging. I realized that I would never be happy working at headquarters, and I discussed my feelings with Jan. Up to that time, all my Bureau experience had consisted of service in a resident agency. Resident agents handled a variety of cases; they were not specialized. Additionally, they had more latitude in determining work priorities. Most important, they also had more frequent and extensive contact with local law enforcement and community leaders than agents assigned to a city headquarters. With this visibility, resident agents were influential in shaping the Bureau's image and reputation. (As I have noted previously, Director Hoover did not share my views concerning the importance of resident agents. He believed them to be necessary evils at best, operating without sufficient direction and control.)

Assignments to resident agencies were the responsibility of the special agent in charge of the field office, subject to the approval of the Administrative Division at FBI headquarters. Each SAC handled the assignment of agents to the resident agencies in different ways. Some staffed the RAs with young agents in order to provide them with the best training experience possible. Other SACs used assignment to a resident agency as a disciplinary measure (for example, agents who were out of favor with the SAC). In my case, I approached, Jack Morley, who had succeeded Scott Werner, and expressed my desire to be placed in an RA. He was extremely receptive to my request, telling me that he would consider it when a vacancy opened up or an RA was expanded. A couple of months later I was summoned to his office. Morley explained that he was thinking about expanding the RA in Colorado Springs because its case load had increased with the growth of the military population (and associated civilian contractors) in the area. Of course, I was ecstatic to hear this and told him enthusiastically that I wanted the assignment. All he said to me was, "Start packing."

CHAPTER 13

THE COLORADO SPRINGS RESIDENT AGENCY

I contacted Jan just as soon as I found out that we would be going to Colorado Springs. She shared my enthusiasm about the transfer, and we began making plans for our move to the city where we met and fell in love. We arrived in Colorado Springs in early May 1970. After getting my family settled in a townhouse in the southeast part of the city, I reported for duty at the RA which occupied two offices on the second floor of the U.S. Post Office building, located in midtown.

The Colorado Springs RA's area of responsibility was the city and El Paso County (a combined population of approximately 235,000 at the time), all of southeastern Colorado to the Kansas border (excluding Pueblo which had its own RA), and five mountain counties to the west. Wally Hague headed the RA; he had replaced Harold Cook, an old timer who had recently retired and would later become a Colorado Springs municipal judge. The RA staff consisted of three special agents; my arrival brought the total to four, including Hague, the senior resident agent.

Hague told me that I would be assigned to the mountain counties (we referred to that area of responsibility as the "mountain" or "western road trip"). I was pleased to hear this because I was very familiar with the area having spent almost three years in Camp Hale training the Tibetan resistance fighters. The mountain road trip encompassed some of the most breathtaking and picturesque scenery in the Rocky Mountains. It included the state penitentiary in Canon City, the state reformatory in Buena Vista, the legendary mining town of Leadville (at 10,152 feet, it's the highest incorporated city in the United States), and the historic former gold camp towns of Cripple Creek and Victor. In addition to the responsibilities of my mountain territory, I would also work some cases originating in Colorado Springs.

I enthusiastically took to all aspects of the mountain road trip. Many of my responsibilities involved the penitentiary and the reformatory, and I developed a good working relationship with officials at both institutions. Whenever I visited, the wardens greeted me personally and granted me numerous privileges. Work at both Canon City and Buena Vista often required me to review inmate records or interview the inmates themselves.

The remainder of my mountain territory caseload largely consisted of tracking down military deserters and other fugitives, conducting background investigations of applicants for federal employment, and trying to locate stolen cars. None of my cases involved a bank robbery. In addition to my investigative responsibilities, I performed important public relations work such as conducting firearms instruction and other training for local police. Along with their obvious practical purpose, these activities were intended to enhance the FBI's image. Indeed, I welcomed opportunities to talk about the Bureau with everyone from town fathers to schoolchildren. On one occasion, my enthusiasm led to considerable embarrassment. I had stopped at a gas station in Leadville. When I handed my credit card to the young attendant, he noticed that it was stamped "FBI-Denver Colorado." He engaged me in conversation, asking questions about the FBI and generally flattering me. The conversation turned to discussing the attributes of a "G-Man" (government man). I enumerated the educational and physical requirements, and the extensive training required. We discussed how the G-Man must be constantly aware of his surroundings and the need to be "street smart." I finally left the station and headed home. About halfway to Buena Vista I noticed an ominous red light flashing behind me. I pulled over and wondered if I had been speeding. Before I could say anything, however, the Colorado State Patrol officer (Sergeant Skip Rodden, whom I knew) approached my vehicle and handed me two items: a gas cap and a credit card. He said, "Cesare, you left the gas cap and the credit card with the young attendant. He very excitedly reported the incident." I humbly accepted the items from Sergeant Rodden and asked him to relay my thanks to the young man and to apologize to him for my absentmindedness.

During my years at Camp Hale with the Tibetans, the Vendome Hotel's restaurant and bar, the Brass Ass Saloon, and other bars in Leadville had provided a bit of relaxation from the daily training grind. I had not seen many of my Leadville friends for over eight years. When I returned as the FBI special agent responsible for the area, they were surprised and pleased. Bob Zaitz, who had operated the bar and restaurant in the Vendome Hotel, was now the mayor. Ann Marie and Joann Bradach were sisters and had been friends with most of the staff at Camp Hale. Both were employed by the Commercial Bank of Leadville. When I returned to the area, Joanne had become the bank's president, and I enjoyed conducting seminars on bank robbery for her.

Another of my friends in Leadville, Fred Van Pelt, was chief of police and descended from a long line of legendary Colorado peace officers. I never hesitated to call on him for assistance. I recall the time that he and I arrested an individual suspected in a stolen vehicle case. We believed his name to be James Earley. The suspect, however, insisted that he was not Earley, but Jay Eastman. When we asked for identification to substantiate his claim, he was unable to produce any. He said that he had been drinking the evening before the arrest, and his wallet and identification had been stolen. The chief and I were not convinced, and we took our suspect to the Leadville police department and interviewed him. He agreed to our fingerprinting him, all the while continuing to deny that he was James Earley and insisting that he was Jay Eastman. We then asked him to sign the fingerprint card. To our amazement, he signed—"James Earley." When we pointed out what he had written, he gave an embarrassed chuckle and admitted that he was really James Earley. He cursed his school training in the Palmer method of cursive penmanship which caused him to unthinkingly and almost automatically write his real name.

Some of my work in Leadville took me to the Climax molybdenum mine located a few miles from the city. The mine was the largest employer in the area and Leadville's economic lifeblood. If one of the miners was the subject of a criminal investigation or a routine background check, the only information I might have about that person was "miner at Climax." For that reason, I had to go to the mine to verify that status, interview him and his coworkers at the mine, or obtain address information from the mine's personnel records to interview him at his home. My contact at the mine was Tim Reynolds who often assisted me during my visits. Tim was one of the many wonderful, cooperative people who made my mountain road trips so enjoyable.

In my Colorado Springs Resident Agency office.
(Author's personal collection)

In the Colorado Springs RA, each agent would be working forty-to-fifty cases at any one time. We had a reputation of being a very active office with numerous bank robberies, extortion and fraud cases, and due to the steadily increasing military population, a large number of cases of desertions and theft of government property.

Once we became involved in a local kidnapping case with a bizarre ending. The kidnapping had occurred in Colorado Springs, and we assisted city police in the investigation. A five-year-old named Gloria Sue Pinter had been abducted at the end of her first day in kindergarten. The abductor, Richard Lee Cunningham, age sixteen and a family friend, was aware that the child's father had recently died. The father, a former member of the U.S. Army had retained his government insurance, and the Pinter family was to collect $10,000 from the policy. Cunningham, assisted by Gloria's eleven-year-old brother, planned to abduct the girl and hold her for $5,000 ransom. Using the pretense that someone was waiting for her, Cunningham approached Gloria in the school yard as she was leaving her kindergarten class. Since she knew Cunningham, she followed him willingly. He then took her to a nearby motel where he murdered her by beating her over the head with a heavy wrench. He hid her body in a drawer of a chest in the motel room. He then called the little girl's mother and told her that he had her daughter and would return her in exchange for $5,000. He also told her not to phone the police or he would kill the child. Frightened, Mrs. Pinter contacted the police, who responded immediately. They conducted interviews, put a tap on the Pinter's phone, and installed a device that would record any subsequent calls. At this point, the police notified our office and I became involved in the case. I was teamed up with Detective Earl Aldrich of the Colorado Springs Police.

Cunningham made two more calls. In the first, he specified that the money was to be dropped off on the east side of Vermijo Park on 26th Street and we placed that area under surveillance. In the next call, however, Cunningham said that the previous arrangement had been a dry run. He gave Gloria's mother new instructions. These called for the money to be left near a vacant field (which turned out to be the third hole on the Valley Hi Golf Course). As soon as we learned of the drop-off point, Detective Aldrich and I positioned ourselves in clumps of foliage under a large tree—close enough to the envelope containing the ransom so that we could observe any attempt to recover it. We remained at this position for well over three hours. Although we kept our conversation in low whispers, I remember telling Earl that it was getting colder as night fell. In a chattering voice, he replied "Tell it to the Red Cross." As the night dragged on, and it got much colder our comments about the temperature progressed from "It's colder than hell" to "I'm freezing my ass off." After one of these exchanges, we heard a rustling noise. I whispered to Earl, "What's that?" He replied "It's just the wind." To our astonishment, a young man suddenly descended from the tree under which we were hiding. He was dressed only in shorts and a tank top. I yelled at him, "Okay Tarzan, what are you doing up in the tree?" He was shaking like a leaf and replied sarcastically, "Freezing my ass off!" He then identified himself as Richard Cunningham. We handcuffed him and turned him over to nearby Colorado Springs police officers who took him to police headquarters for questioning. Cunningham was found guilty of the crime and sentenced to two life terms in the Colorado State Penitentiary where he is still incarcerated (as of this writing). The victim's brother received probation because of his youth.

After the kidnapper's arrest, I told Aldrich that I didn't think his comment about the Red Cross had caused Cunningham to come down from the tree. Even so, we had in fact frozen him out instead of smoking him out! He was apparently a lot colder than we were. Years later, I was asked to say a few words on behalf of Detective Aldrich at his retirement ceremony. Naturally, I related the tale that I called "You, Me, and the Guy in the Tree." Evidently enjoying the story, the audience laughed.

I continued mountain rounds for about six years. During this time, in 1972, I attended an FBI in-service school which qualified me to handle incidents involving bombs and give instruction on that subject to police agencies within the Colorado Springs RA's area of responsibility. Shortly after attending the bomb course, I was designated a general police instructor which qualified me to instruct local police, civilian groups, and military units in numerous law enforcement subjects, including bomb handling, firearms training, legal matters (e.g., probable cause), search and seizure, arrest techniques, and current criminal trends.

I was very comfortable at this stage of my career. I worked with capable local law enforcement officers and enjoyed considerable independence. And I was fearless (because I didn't know any better!)—eager to match my wits with the bad-guy halfwits I was up against.

Much of my mountain work concerned deserters. I recall arresting a young man who was working on a ranch in the San Luis Valley. He was most unhappy being arrested, ranting and raving at the absurdity of making a federal case out of what was in his view a minor offense. He continued his protest all the way to the county jail, and then finally admitted that he was sick and tired of ranch work and was looking forward to "changing jobs."

Deserter apprehensions were always fun and exciting, and at times, relatively easy. However, I always approached these cases cautiously because deserters, like any other fugitives on the run, might take drastic measures to evade capture when cornered. One fugitive, an Army deserter, attempted to escape by jumping out of a side window on the ground floor of the rooming house in Manitou Springs, Colorado, where he lived. But, when he saw FBI agents at the rear of the building, he quickly reentered the side window and jumped head first through an open front window, only to find my partner and me waiting for him. While I was returning him to the custody of military police (MPs), he asked how many agents had been at the scene of his arrest. I asked him why he wanted to know. He replied, "Everywhere I looked there seemed to be FBI agents." When we handed him over to the MPs, he disgustedly remarked, "Dammit! And to think I watched the FBI show on TV last night, and I rooted for you guys!"

Sometimes, in apprehending a deserter, we encountered his employer. On one occasion, the operator of a Colorado Springs garbage collection company was extremely irritated when we arrested a young deserter who worked for his company. According to the man, the fugitive was one of the best and most polite "G-Men" he had ever employed. I handcuffed our polite "G-Man" and ignored the wise-ass comparison.

When I was an FBI agent, bank robberies were the centerpieces of Bureau investigations. To be assigned to the bank robbery squad at a city headquarters office meant that the agent was regarded as mature, capable, and highly respected by both his supervisors and peers. Resident agencies, however, did not have specialized bank robbery units; agents took turns at handling those cases. Although no bank robberies occurred in my mountain area of responsibility, I became involved in several of those cases occurring in and around Colorado Springs.

For some reason, bank robberies always seemed to occur on Friday afternoons, which usually screwed up your weekend. Also, most bank robberies were nonviolent. Bank robbers tended to be young and emotionally unstable, looking for a "big score" that would solve a personal problem. Usually, the robber demanded cash from a bank teller either verbally or with a note handed over the counter. Robbers rarely used guns, but sometimes would keep a hand inside a coat or pants to suggest that they had one. Although fairly easy to commit, most holdups, contrary to popular belief, netted relatively small amounts of money, normally less than $2,000.

Bank robbers, in my experience, were not "rocket scientists." More than once on cases that I worked, the robber presented a demand note written on the back of a personal check which bore the robber's name and address! Psychologists might say this was a plea for help—the robber wanted to be caught. My view is that it was just stupidity. On one occasion I responded to a bank robbery in Colorado Springs which had occurred late on a Friday afternoon. When I arrived at the scene, the police had already bagged the perpetrator, a young punk, along with the bank loot. He was taken to police headquarters for questioning. I egged him on by saying we got your ass dead center. He replied, "My ass you do!" I said we had two great eyewitnesses who could ID him. He responded, "Bullshit! Who are they?" I said the two young bank tellers who got a good look at you. He said, "No way—I had my ski mask on the whole time I was in the bank."

Sometimes robbers would meet up with a feisty bank teller. One time, I was called to investigate an aborted holdup of one of the local banks. It seemed the robber had entered the bank and pushed a demand note across the counter to a female teller and ordered her to give him all the twenties she had. She shoved the note back to the would-be robber and yelled, "Hit the road jerk!" whereupon the robber made a hasty exit. Although the teller gave an excellent description of the robber, I was never able to identify or apprehend him. In another case, a robber entered a bank located in the north section of Colorado Springs and gave a young female teller a one hundred-dollar bill. While she was making change as requested by the bandit, he shoved a paper bag across the counter, thrusting his hand underneath his light jacket at the same time to make it appear that he was armed. The bag contained a note: "Make one bad move, and I'll kill you. Fill the bag and don't speak or move for five minutes. After I leave, one of my men will be watching you." The teller began filling the bag with assorted coins which irritated the bank robber. He shouted, "You numb nuts—fill it with large bills, NO coins!" She turned to him and threw the bag of coins in his direction and screamed, "He's no customer; he's a bank robber!" She then dropped to the floor and pushed the alarm. The frustrated bank robber, caught by surprise, fled the bank. Responding police officers apprehended him a short distance from the bank. In his haste to depart, he had left his one hundred-dollar bill behind.

Sometimes bank robberies took me out of state. Once, I was subpoenaed to appear at the trial of a bank robber in Jefferson City, Missouri. The robbery had taken place in Missouri, and the bank robber had been apprehended in Colorado Springs. At the trial the testimony of a fingerprint expert from the FBI laboratory in Washington, D. C., preceded mine. His testimony was extremely damaging to the defendant's case. The defense attorney attempted to discredit the fingerprint expert's testimony, but his cross examination only brought out more information damaging to his client. The defense attorney was frustrated, exasperated, agitated, and thoroughly ineffective. Finally, deciding not to dig the hole any deeper, he turned to the judge and said, "That's all I have your honor." The prosecution then called me to the stand. I identified myself, stated that I had been with the Bureau for twelve years, and described the circumstances of the arrest in Colorado Springs. The prosecutor then related that he had nothing further for the witness. I turned my attention to the defense attorney; I thought he would go up and down my testimony like a lawn mower. I prepared myself for the worst. It was hot in the courtroom, and I began to sweat. The defense attorney got up from his table, approached me in the witness box, leaned over and said in an annoying manner, "Mr. Cesare how is Mr. Hoover?" I said, "Fine counselor." He turned to the judge and said, "That's all, your honor."

In the Colorado Springs resident agency, the agents took turns pulling weekend duty. On one of my turns, the Colorado Springs police notified me that there had been a break-in at the National Guard Armory. The burglar had been caught with several guns and ammo stolen from the armory. I interviewed the suspect, a young man, in connection with the theft. I recalled that about a week before a large theft of weapons and ammo had taken place in the Denver area. As I questioned the suspect, I pointed out that the two burglaries were similar in MO (modus operandi) and it looked like he might have been responsible for the Denver job. He hesitated, took a deep breath, and very indignantly stated, "Mr. Cesare, I'm not big time—I'm just a nickel-and-dime burglar!"

CHAPTER 14

SENIOR RESIDENT AGENT

After six years on the mountain road trip, in October 1976 I became the senior resident agent (SRA) in Colorado Springs. I believe that my seniority and experience were important reasons for my selection to the post. Although I had no formal authority over the other five agents then assigned to the RA and the job mostly amounted to administration and coordination, I must admit that I was pleased with the designation. In the event of a major case originating in the Colorado Springs area, I would be the agent in charge. As SRA, I was also responsible for maintaining a high profile in our area and was expected to have close contact with influential figures in the community (e.g., business leaders, media representatives, politicians, and military and law enforcement officials). I diligently cultivated these relationships and felt that my efforts reflected favorably on the Colorado Springs RA and the FBI generally.

By the time I became the SRA, Colorado Springs had experienced phenomenal growth. When I first visited the city in late 1959, while with the CIA, its population was roughly 70,000. When Jan and I returned in May 1970 with my assignment to the RA, the city's population had nearly doubled to 135,000 (235,000 including all of El Paso County). Much of the growth was due to the increasing importance of the area's military installations—Ent Air Force Base, Peterson Air Force Base, the North American Air Defense Command (NORAD), the U.S. Air Force Academy, and Fort Carson—with their large military populations and associated civilian contractors.

I was especially pleased to be working more closely with the Colorado Springs Police Department. It was a very professional organization with excellent personnel. (During my tenure as SRA, it was rated in the top 100 departments in the country.) The department had a large area to patrol because of the city's rapid growth and did so efficiently, effectively, and ethically. My Bureau instructors had always taught me that cooperation was the backbone of law enforcement. I adhered faithfully to this axiom in dealing with local police and sheriff's departments as well as other law enforcement agencies. We in the Bureau knew that we were only as good as the information we received—information that came mostly from local law enforcement. I always tried to give something back in return for their help. As SRA I also made it known that it did not matter to me which agency—local or federal—got the credit for solving a case.

One of the first issues I confronted as SRA was to relocate the resident agency's offices. For almost ten years we had been located in a building in an industrial/commercial area which was not very accessible to the public. Nor was the building itself up to Bureau standards. I wrote several letters to the Government Services Administration via our SAC in Denver requesting to be relocated. Finally, we were able to move to a professional building located in midtown Colorado Springs.

Due to the RA's close proximity to Fort Carson, we had a large number of deserter cases; quite a few of these fugitives hid out in Manitou Springs, a small town a few miles west of Colorado Springs. During part of the period I served in the RA, Manitou Springs was a haven for what were then called "hippies" or "flower children." Essentially, they were nonconformists. We suspected that deserters found refuge in some of the houses inhabited by the "hippies." It got to the point that whenever one of us went to Manitou Springs, that agent would return with a deserter in custody. Often, deserters would find low-paying jobs in the town as musicians, cooks, handymen or other laborers. As a result, some employers in Manitou Springs, like the hippies, hated to see us arrive because it usually meant that that one of their employees and new-found friends would be arrested. In one case, I took into custody an Army deserter who was one of the members of a musical trio that was performing in a local bar. The group's name had given me an only too obvious lead—"The Fugitives."

You never knew what to expect when the phone rang at the RA. One time I received a call from an obviously inebriated individual who excitedly complained that his automobile had been broken into and that someone had stolen the steering wheel, brake pedal, and dashboard. I was about to tell him that he should report the theft to the Colorado Springs police when the tipsy man said, "I'm sorry Mr. FBI," and loudly added "I got in the back seat by mistake."

Some phone calls, of course, were deadly serious. I distinctly recall my first kidnapping case as the SRA. A call came from the Manitou Springs police who informed me that eighteen-year-old Lori Mestas had been abducted from the Elk-O Motel operated by her parents. We responded immediately. The Manitou Springs police told us that the perpetrator, who did not use a gun, had tied up the young woman's parents and had abducted Lori when he did not find enough money in the motel office. He told the parents that he would hold Lori for ransom. He also took the Mestas' vehicle, a Chevrolet sedan. I was accompanied by two capable fellow agents, Carl Shepherd and Don Kusulas; we resolved to get the girl back to her parents. Assisted by the Manitou Springs police, we began an intensive investigation, sending out leads to state and national law enforcement agencies.

We took several other actions in our effort to find the girl. We conducted an air search in the immediate and surrounding areas for the stolen vehicle, but failed to locate it. We convinced Manuel Mestas, Lori's father, to make a television plea to encourage the kidnapper to contact either the police or the family. He was uncertain about what to say so I wrote the statement he read on television. We even used a Colorado Springs psychiatrist, who specialized in working with emotionally troubled criminals, to appeal to the kidnapper to think, not act. Apparently, one of these techniques worked. The family received a call from their daughter who said her kidnapper was demanding $6,000 in ransom; the money was to be placed in a telephone booth in New Orleans. As a result of this information, an intensive search ensued. The girl and her kidnapper were located at a motel in Metairie, Louisiana, a suburb of New Orleans. Lori was freed and returned to her parents six days after she had been abducted. Charles Draper, a classmate of mine at the FBI Academy headed the team that made the rescue. The kidnapper, identified as Don Wesley Hartline, a white male, age thirty-three, was taken into federal custody. On

April 20, 1979, Hartline was convicted in federal district court in Denver on a charge of kidnapping and sentenced to ten and one-half years in federal prison.

United States Department of Justice
UNITED STATES ATTORNEY
DISTRICT OF COLORADO

CRIMINAL DIVISION
C-336 U.S. COURTHOUSE, DRAWER 3615
DENVER, COLORADO 80294
COMMERCIAL TELEPHONE (303) 837-2081
FTS: 327-2081

CIVIL DIVISION
674 FEDERAL BUILDING, DRAWER 3615
DENVER, COLORADO 80294
COMMERCIAL TELEPHONE (303) 837-2065
FTS: 327-2065

May 9, 1979

Jack N. Egnor
Special Agent in Charge
Federal Bureau of Investigation
P.O. Box 1229
Denver, Colorado 80201

Re: United States v. Don Wesley Hartline
      Criminal No. 79-CR-9

Dear Sir:

I would like to take this opportunity to commend Special Agent Don Cesare for his highly professional, conscientious and thorough work in the case of United States v. Don Wesley Hartline, Criminal No. 79-CR-9. Mr. Hartline was convicted on April 20, 1979, of kidnapping Lori Mestas from her home in Colorado Springs.

This case necessitated the investigation of many leads, combining the talents of a number of FBI agents and Mr. Cesare used these talents to the best interests of the government. The investigative expertise exhibited throughout this case by Mr. Cesare was invaluable to a successful prosecution.

It was a pleasure to work with Mr. Cesare in this case.

Very truly yours,

JOSEPH DOLAN
United States Attorney

By: SUSAN R. ROBERTS
Assistant United States Attorney

SEARCHED_____ INDEXED_____
SERIALIZED_____ FILED_____
MAY 1 4 1979
FBI — DENVER
CESARE

Letter from U.S. attorney commending author for his work on Lori Mestas kidnapping case. (Author's personal collection)

As a result of my work on the Mestas kidnapping, I was selected to attend in-service training in SWAT (Special Weapons and Tactics) and, on completion, was appointed SWAT team leader for the Denver office. Although I never led the team on an operation, our preparation enabled us to acquire what we referred to as "adventure training." We snow skied extensively at many of the Colorado ski areas, operated with Colorado wildlife officers on snowmobiles and horseback, and trained with the military at Fort Carson. The Army instructed our group in rappelling, and allowed us to use its "combat village" replica to familiarize ourselves with the techniques involved in house-to-house searches. Also, in cooperation with airline officials and the management of the Colorado Springs airport, we practiced on different types of aircraft dealing with problems that might arise with a plane on the ground.

Author in SWAT training in Colorado mountains.
(Author's personal collection)

Another type of phone call—those notifying me that a bomb threat had been made to a commercial aircraft—also got my complete attention. Such calls often came in the middle of the night, waking me from a deep sleep. In these incidents, airline officials had been told that the bomb was a pressure device set to explode when the plane descended below 5,000 feet. Since the elevation of the Colorado Springs Municipal Airport was 6,187 feet, these flights would be diverted from their original destinations and directed to land in Colorado Springs.

In one of these cases in early February 1985, a United Airlines flight bound from San Francisco to Honolulu was diverted to Colorado Springs because of a bomb threat. An anonymous caller told United officials that a package on the plane would explode when the flight descended below 5,000 feet. I received notification of the incident from the Colorado Springs police; Neil Stratton, the department's chief and several other officers were responding. I hurried out to the airport and was met by Ed Stricker, the airport manager, and some of his staff. Chief Stratton and his officers soon joined us on the tarmac in front of the passenger terminal. It was a bitterly cold winter night and we uncomfortably and impatiently awaited the arrival of UAL 727. Soon the plane appeared, made a direct approach, landed, and taxied a short distance to a complete stop. The pilot shut down the engines, and our group jumped into several police vehicles and headed for the aircraft. We were accompanied by an airport crew that placed a portable passenger stairway at the plane's front door. I quickly ran up the stairs and was confronted by a man in a UAL uniform. I excitedly said to him, "I'm Don Cesare with the FBI, how can I help you?" He answered, "You can take this!" and shoved a package into my chest. I instinctively turned and headed down the stairs. I suddenly realized that this package contained the bomb, and I was carrying it! I was scared to death and sick to my stomach. As I descended the stairs I thought what the hell do I do with this? I approached Chief Stratton and several of his officers, but they hurriedly backed away from me, with the chief yelling, "Get rid of that damn thing!" Not knowing what else to do, I ran as fast as I could down the runway away from the aircraft, holding onto the package carefully. My heart was pounding so hard that I thought it would come through my rib cage. All I could think of was that the bomb might explode any moment, and that I had been an idiot for getting myself into such a situation. After what seemed like an eternity of running, I stopped and gingerly laid the package down and double-timed it back to the group as fast as my legs would carry me. I arrived breathless and completely exhausted. My friends were very happy to see me still in one piece, but couldn't help questioning my sanity. Finally, the EOD (Explosives Ordnance Disposal) team from Fort Carson arrived. Their examination revealed the package to contain a harmless device made of wooden dowels wrapped in dynamite paper and attached to a simulated timer. After this bizarre incident, I can assure you that in future cases involving bombs I was considerably more cautious.

In my years as SRA, I valued highly the importance of good relations with the Colorado Springs community. Its citizens evidently felt comfortable with the FBI; they inundated me with questions. I particularly recall the following letter:

Mr. Cesare,

My name is Tommy Scott, and I am 10 years old. I am writing a paper about the great FBI for our school social studies class. So I would like you to please send me 10 of your most wanted posters. Thank you. And when I am old enough I might become one myself.

Yours truly,
Tommy Scott

I always tried to respond to requests like this and to any others I received as best I could. I also made myself visible by speaking to various civic organizations and by conducting a variety of law enforcement schools and other training. As time passed and the threat from international and domestic terrorism increased, the Bureau gave combating it a high priority and I began to emphasize the subject in my public presentations.

I enjoyed my role in the RA, felt comfortable in my position, and in our relations with the Colorado Springs community. This did not mean that there wasn't a bump or two along the road during my tour. The Denver office had a particularly aggressive and ambitious assistant special agent in charge (ASAC) with whom I clashed occasionally, resulting in me usually coming out on the short end of the stick. The confrontations were normally over transferring personnel in and out of the RA. I believe these disagreements led to his growing animosity toward me and that it would only be a matter of time before he would nail me for some infraction or another and have *me* transferred.

On one unforgettable occasion, I managed to get the upper hand on the ASAC. A service club in Colorado Springs asked me if the special agent in charge of the Denver office would address the group on the responsibilities of that position. The speaking date, unfortunately, coincided with the SAC's annual trip to Washington, D.C. The service club settled for my administrative nemesis, the ASAC, who had the personality of a bag of rocks. Following his speech at the service club's luncheon, the ASAC asked if there were any questions. An audience member raised his hand and complained that he thought the Colorado Springs resident agents were antisocial. The ASAC looked directly at me, and I thought, "This guy will use this as an excuse to deep-six me." I was ready to call the Mayflower movers. He then asked the questioner what he meant by "antisocial"? The man replied, "Well, I live near Don Cesare, and I know that he leaves for work before the neighborhood is up and comes home late every night—I think that's antisocial!" His response, of course, made my day and also unwittingly extended my tenure in the Colorado Springs RA. Shortly after this episode the ASAC was transferred from the Denver office. I attended his farewell party, but only because I was so happy to see him go.

During the latter period of my service as SRA in Colorado Springs, I became heavily involved in the FBI's counter intelligence program (Foreign Counter Intelligence, or FCI, as we called it). The FCI program protected the United States against foreign intelligence operations and espionage, and accomplished its mission by interacting with local law enforcement and elements of the U.S. intelligence community.

My FCI supervisor in the Denver office was Tom Howard. He was an innovator, well-suited for his role. His enthusiasm was infectious as he described to me how he planned to revitalize the Denver office's FCI program. While agents in the Denver office would be involved, he wanted the Colorado Springs RA to take the lead because of the numerous military installations in its area of responsibility. Foreign intelligence agencies would be eager to exploit military personnel on those bases. The FBI saw that attraction as an opportunity to turn the tables by employing U.S. military personnel in a counterintelligence role. The Bureau was prohibited from using military personnel in its intelligence operations, but the FBI could participate in the military's intelligence activities. By partnering with the military, Howard explained, the FBI could influence assignments given to these intelligence assets and participate in their debriefings. The Bureau would not recruit these operatives; that would be the military's responsibility.

In carrying out this program I dealt extensively with the Air Force's Office of Special Investigations and with Army intelligence agents. They recruited assets from local military installations and groomed them for intelligence activities. Although I had no part in recruiting these operatives, I was present when they were assigned intelligence targets and objectives. The intelligence operation usually involved the asset making contact with foreign nationals in the embassies, consulates, and visiting delegations from the Soviet Union, Cuba, and the People's Republic of China. Some of the operations were successful; some were not.

Another aspect of an RA's intelligence activity consisted of surveillance work. Groups or individuals from targeted countries would periodically tour the United States, usually under the auspices of cultural exchange programs. The groups would often include an intelligence agent who had no obvious function within the group, except to keep an eye on the others, prevent defections, and pick up any useful information he or she might come across. The FBI, normally agents from an RA, kept these groups under surveillance. An RA was also alerted when embassy or consulate personnel from a targeted country traveled through its area. Agents from the RA were required to report who these individuals contacted and any places they visited.

One of my memorable experiences with this type of surveillance occurred when the RA was alerted to the impending travel of a known GRU agent (the GRU, or Main Intelligence Directorate, was the USSR's and still is Russia's largest intelligence agency). The targeted individual (called "the package") had arrived in Denver at Stapleton Airport (then the city's major airport), rented a car, spent two nights in a nearby motel, and visited several tourist sites in and around Denver. During this period, Denver FBI agents had him under constant surveillance. On the morning of the third day, the Denver agents notified our RA by radio that "the package" was heading south on Interstate Highway 25 and told us to take over the operation and continue the surveillance. Our RA team consisted of two cars and three agents— me in one car and Carl Shepherd and Don Kusulas in the other. We picked up the surveillance just south of Castle Rock, about halfway to Colorado Springs. We were surprised that "the package" did not stop when he reached Colorado Springs (a city full of military installations and defense contractors) but continued south toward Pueblo. I radioed ahead to Steve Markardt of the Pueblo RA and asked him to assist in the surveillance. Markardt agreed and I told Shepherd and Kasulas to head back to Colorado Springs.

Markardt and I, each in separate cars, followed the GRU agent who exited I-25 and headed east on U.S. Highway 50 toward La Junta, Colorado, about sixty-five miles east of Pueblo. In La Junta, he checked into a motel and stayed the night, checking out the next day late in the morning. As he was checking out, he had a short conversation with the desk clerk who told us he had asked directions to the "Indian Museum" (the Koshare Indian Kiva and Museum) located just outside La Junta. We trailed him there. After he entered, I followed him in and shadowed him through the museum while Steve waited outside. I had never been to the museum before and became so interested in its exhibits that I suddenly realized I had lost track of "the package." I hurriedly turned the corner of a display and bumped right into him. We were both startled by the sudden encounter, but I was prepared. In my best Italian I said "Scusa per favore." He made no reply and we both resumed touring the museum. After several hours in the museum, "the package" returned to his car and continued east to the Colorado-Kansas border. In Holly, Colorado, near the border, we met Kansas City agents who picked up the surveillance and we terminated ours. Other than the incident in museum, the surveillance had been uneventful. To this day, I'm not sure "the package" bought my response in Italian to our bumping into one another, but I do remember the frightened look he had on his face.

After I retired from the FBI, foreign intelligence gathering took place in my own home. In the summer of 1987 officials of the U. S. Olympic Committee contacted Jan, who is of Serbian descent, and asked if she would host members of the Czechoslovakian cycling team for an evening at our home. They were housed at the Olympic Training Center in Colorado Springs and were to compete in a cycling event at the Air Force Academy sponsored by the U.S. Cycling Federation. On the designated night the group, consisting of Slovenians, arrived. Jan had arranged for a few people of Czechoslovakian descent from her hometown of Pueblo, Colorado, to join us. The cycling team consisted of eight riders and two coaches, and they mixed well with our visitors from Pueblo. During the evening's conversations we discovered that one of the two coaches was, indeed, the team coach. However, the other individual, known to us as Igor, was quite probably the political officer assigned to the team. Igor consumed large amounts of vodka and asked many questions of the Pueblo contingent—questions about prices, salaries (although most were retired), and their political views regarding Czechoslovakia. Strangely, what seemed to impress the cyclists and coaches most was the fact that many of our supermarkets were open twenty-four hours a day!

In 1985 my FBI career came to an end. In May I received a letter from the Bureau's personnel department which notified me that the provisions of Public Law 93-35 required a federal law enforcement agent with at least twenty years of service to be separated on the last day of the month in which he or she turned fifty-five (too young I thought). My mandatory retirement date was July 31, 1985. I really did not want to leave. I enjoyed my job and felt that I could continue to be an effective SRA for at least five more years. But that was the law, and I had no option but to retire. My impending retirement caused me to look back fondly on my many exciting and interesting years in the Bureau. I always felt that I was fortunate to have been a part of and have made contributions to an organization made up of individuals with the highest standards who, like me, were proud of and loyal to the finest law enforcement agency in the world.

CHAPTER 15

Donald J. Cesare (Retired)
Federal Bureau of Investigation

AFTER THE FBI

After their retirement, many former FBI agents continued to use the training and skills acquired during their years of service. I decided to put my expertise from conducting law enforcement schools for the Bureau to work. Along with initiative, resourcefulness, and persistence—all standard equipment in an agent's personal makeup—I faced retirement with a positive attitude.

In January 1986 the U.S. Department of Justice initiated the International Criminal Investigative Training and Assistance Program (ICITAP) to improve, through training, criminal investigative capabilities in Central and South America, and the Caribbean. The initiative supported broader U.S. policy goals that encouraged indigenous efforts to improve the administration of justice and to strengthen the infrastructure of democracy throughout the Western Hemisphere. Miranda Associates, Inc., a Washington D.C. firm, ran the program under a contract with the Justice Department. If I joined up, I would be one of many retired agents already working in the program. I would be a part-time consultant and would be required to travel overseas. I discussed the job with Jan, and she agreed I should accept the position.

My first assignment with Miranda Associates was to make a presentation to elements of El Salvador's National Police Force and several high-ranking members of its National Guard at the National Police Headquarters in San Salvador, the capital. My remarks covered how to investigate extortion and kidnapping cases and prepare them for prosecution. Only Italy and some countries in the Middle East exceeded El Salvador in these types of cases. In my opening remarks, I included the law enforcement code of ethics published by the International Association of Chiefs of Police. I believed this would emphasize the importance of considering human rights in police work and instill in each attendee a sense of professionalism. Miranda Associates received excellent comments on my presentation.

For over three years, I traveled throughout Central and South America and the Caribbean teaching major crimes investigation in ICITAP courses, as well as numerous other police programs, to over 1,300 high-ranking police officers in 18 countries. The courses covered the management of criminal investigations, including initial investigation, case screening, continuing investigation, police-prosecutor relations, police ethics, and monitoring factors such as motive, opportunity, and other evidence associated with a crime.

While working in the ICITAP in Central America, I witnessed several shootings and was near the scene of a few bombings. With the exception of Belize and Costa Rica, Central America was then in constant turmoil. An incident I vividly recall occurred during my second trip to El Salvador in 1989. Following a presentation to a group of Salvadoran police, I was invited to lunch by a police official who had not been in the class. The restaurant he took me to was located on a hilltop overlooking a ravine on the outskirts of San Salvador. Our table was near the ravine's edge and was buffered by some waist-high foliage. As we were finishing lunch, gunfire coming from the ravine startled us. About a dozen people, all firing rifles, were advancing toward a white-painted building located near the end of the ravine. The occupants of the building responded with what sounded like automatic weapons fire which caused the attackers to cease firing and retreat hastily. Shocked, I turned to my host for an explanation. He casually explained that the building housed a phone company protected by the Democratic Resistance Forces, then in power in El Salvador. The attackers belonged to the Farabundo Marti National Liberation Front, a leftist organization whose objective was to overthrow the government and install a Communist regime. They hoped to achieve their goal by disrupting or destroying the country's infrastructure, hence the attack on the phone company. On our return to the city, I thanked my host for the information he had provided on the country's political situation, but expressed my disbelief at what I had just witnessed—a firefight between forces from warring political groups. I assured him it was an episode I would never forget!

All in all, working for ICITAP was a challenging and rewarding experience. However, the years of extensive travel began to take their toll, and I became less enthusiastic about my job. Jan remarked that she had seen more of me when I was with the FBI. After careful consideration, I decided to terminate my contract. The program administrator was very unhappy with my decision, but I remained firm. To show the proper spirit I gave him copies of the lesson plans I had used in my presentations.

Even though I had relinquished the position as a consultant with the ICITAP, I continued as an investigator under contract with the Department of Defense (DoD). I had been performing investigations for DoD on and off for several years. The cases assigned to me were usually background investigations of individuals seeking security clearances. Because the investigations required interviews in residential areas, they were known as "doorbell" cases. They involved interviewing the subject's coworkers and neighbors, conducting credit and criminal checks, and developing various other sources of information. Officials in Washington, D.C. decided whether to grant the security clearance, but based their decision largely on the investigative report.

I had used the DoD background investigations as fill-ins during gaps in my overseas assignments with ICITAP. After leaving that program, I devoted full time to these cases, and they continued to occupy me for several more years. As most concerned employees of the aerospace industry in the Denver area, I worked with such firms as Martin Marietta, Lockheed, and McDonnell Douglas, so much so that I was on a first-name basis with many of their executives. Each background investigation had to be completed and a written report submitted by a deadline. As with the extensive traveling for ICITAP, these deadlines, the almost daily trips to Denver from Colorado Springs, and the never-ending knocking on doors began to wear on me.

The negative effects of the investigative work made me think about retiring completely. As I mulled this over, officials from the Colorado Department of Corrections contacted me and asked if I would be interested in working part-time for that agency. Would travel be involved? Would there be deadlines to meet? Would I have to go door-to-door conducting interviews? These questions sprang immediately to my mind. The answer to each was a resounding *no*. The work involved interviews (called "integrity" interviews) of Department of Corrections job applicants. Using information the prospective employee had provided on his or her application, the interviewer would pose a series of questions, and based on the responses, would make a judgment regarding the applicant's honesty and reliability.

I accepted the position; it was a good decision because I truly enjoyed the work. I interviewed hundreds of applicants and met some interesting people—from wardens to guards, from cooks to clerks to administrators. I worked for the Department of Corrections for five years until 2003 when I decided it was time to retire permanently. Corrections officials pressed me hard to stay. I wanted to know why, and they replied that in addition to my having done a good job, they believed that no one lied to a retired FBI agent. Although I didn't comment, after five years of conducting "integrity" interviews, I knew better!

AFTERWORD

As I reflect on my career, I can't but be grateful to the trio of agencies that so profoundly affected my life and my achievements. The Marine Corps taught me the importance of discipline and stressed the significance of leadership. It not only helped me to develop these qualities but also continually drove me to fulfill my potential. In essence my experiences as a Marine Corps officer matured me and taught me to strive for excellence in any undertaking.

In the CIA, I entered the arcane world of intelligence, participated in covert activities, and found the adventures I had been seeking. My associates were all fiercely aggressive individuals who achieved their goals with a tenacious work ethic, creative approaches to problems, and willingness to take risks.

In the FBI I fulfilled my father's wish for me and my own ambition. In more than twenty years' service with the Bureau, I learned how to deal with people. I was also an eyewitness to and a direct participant in events of historic importance. I recognize most people do not have such opportunities and am humbled by that.

The Marine Corps, CIA, and FBI all reinforced my senses of loyalty and patriotism. I am extremely proud to have been able to serve my country and the State of Colorado in all three for well over forty years.

ACKNOWLEDGEMENTS

I want especially to thank my wife, Jan, for her love, support, and encouragement throughout my career. I am also deeply indebted to Duane Reed, former archivist at the U. S. Air Force Academy, who urged me to write this book and guided my efforts. Thanks go as well to Elliott Converse, a retired Air Force colonel and professional historian, for editing the manuscript and offering useful suggestions for improving it. I am particularly grateful to Leslie Lethbridge who generously, skillfully, and rapidly transformed my handwritten manuscript into digital form.

I am especially indebted to Dave Rickert who has provided immeasurable service in the preparation of the book for publication.

In addition I want to thank my friends Guenther Polok, Jim Oberhofer, and Peter Blaney for their continuing interest and invaluable support of the project.

About the Type

BLUE · GRAY · BLACK
MY SERVICE TO COUNTRY
is set in *Adobe Minion Pro*.

Minion is an old style serif typeface inspired by letters used during the late Renaissance-era. It was designed in 1990 by Robert Slimbach for Adobe Systems. It has proven to be a popular and adaptive type, used for everything from Stieg Larsson's Millennium Trilogy to other languages including Arabic, Cyrillic, Hebrew, Thai, and Song (Chinese). Minion is noted for its versatility, warmth and balance, making it one of the most readable and widely-used fonts available today.

Have you seen
our other
Rhyolite Press
Publications . . ?

Visit Rhyolite Press
www.RhyolitePress.com

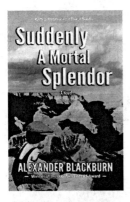

East of the Mountains
and West of the Sun

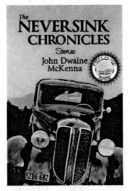

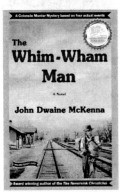

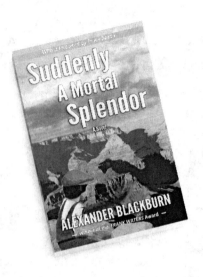

SUDDENLY A MORTAL SPLENDOR

A NOVEL BY

ALEXANDER BLACKBURN

Ultimately, what Alexander Blackburn's Suddenly a Mortal Splendor offers readers is a radical, grounded sense of optimism. Blackburn and his fictional counterpart Paul Szabo are survivors, and from a survivor's standpoint, nuclear blasts can be willed to reveal an underside of beauty. Catastrophe, mass destruction, human cruelty and depravity—this, and we, can only be made meaningful by narrating these events into other patterns and fictions, imagining alternative cause and effect chains which steer us away from oblivion and toward less cataclysmic non-fictional realities.

$16.95 at bookstores everywhere, or direct from the publisher:
www.rhyolitepress.com

ISBN 978-0-9896763-6-6

Praise for: Suddenly A Mortal Splendor

Alexander Blackburn is one of the most important writers in the American West today.

— Bloomsbury Review

Suddenly A Mortal Splendor is elegantly built, in its leanness of thought and in the clear-lined prose ahat flows from a breadth of cool intelligence and warm human feeling.

— Reynolds Price

Beautiful, intelligent and wonderfully crafted, an important book that will last.

— Bret Lott

Beautifully crafted, frequently moving tale about innocence and greed as they play out in the lives of citizens and in the lives of empires.

— The Dallas Morning News

Blackburn tears off great hunk of late 20th century history to use as a source of inspiration and moral instruction with savage humor about man's limitless capacity for inhumanity and equally limitless capacity for survival.

— Boston Globe

A wonderful story. I read it with fascination.

— Bill Henderson, Pushcart Press

A dynamic novel, fast paced and loaded with deeply resonating character.

— Santa Fe New Mexican

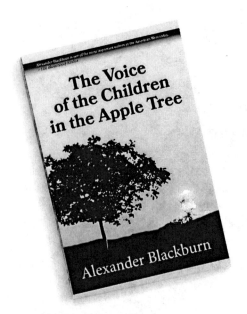

The Voice
of the Children
in the Apple Tree

by

Alexander Blackburn

Alexander Blackburn is one of the most important writers in the American West today. —The Bloomsbury Review

This major novel offers a vision of hope for the future: Citation of Alexander Blackburn's *The Voice of the Children in the Apple Tree* for the International PeaceWriting Award.

$18.95 at bookstores everywhere, or direct from the publisher:
www.rhyolitepress.com

ISBN 978-0-9896763-2-8

The Voice
of the Children
in the Apple Tree

The love of a New England heiress who becomes a public nurse and of a country boy from the south and southwest who becomes an atomic physicist spans half of the twentieth century and culminates in their repudiation of the decision to use the atomic bombs against Japan in the Second World War. The shared conscience and intrepid compassion of Trinc and Aeneas reveal the inter-connectedness of life, the refuge of a new world of consciousness, and the hope for recovered innocence, one suggested by T.S. Eliot's imagery, "The voice of the children in the apple tree." This epic novel braids the lives of highly individual, brightly vivid characters into the history of their times. It is a love story for the ages that takes place in the shadow of the atomic bomb.

The atomic bomb is a turning point in world history. Both Trinc and Aeneas are closely involved in historical events, inseparable from them, and the vicissitudes they endure are those ingrained in the times they live through. They are terrific characterizations! *The Voice of the Children in the Apple Tree* is large, the event momentous, and the perspective always fitting. Here is another real triumph.

—Fred Chappell, Poet Laureate of North Carolina

The Door
of the
Sad People

by Alexander Blackburn

The Door of the Sad People is one of the most remarkable books I have read, ever. It caught me pleasurably off guard at almost every turn.

> —Fred Chappell - Recipient of the Bollingen Prize for Poetry, Yale University

$16.95 at bookstores everywhere, or direct from the publisher:
www.rhyolitepress.com

ISBN 978-0-9896763-4-2

THE DOOR OF THE SAD PEOPLE is a coming-of-age story that takes place against the background of the Colorado coalmining wars long-remembered for the Ludlow Massacre of 1914. Visionary, the novel traces the tyrannous countenance of a corporate society to its origins in humankind's "sad" limitations and flaws.

Young Tree Penhallow escapes an abusive father and an attempted murder but finds a surrogate father in "Kill Devil" Dare, a friend in Mother Jones, "the miners' angel," and a home in a loving, once-patrician Hispanic family now eking out a hard scrable life through farming and mining. When his adoptive family is almost entirely exterminated by militia during a strike, a spiritual "door" opens, confirming for Tree the eternal truth of compassion, how it holds humanity together.

Tree Penhallow matures into an artist and hero who confronts the violent and perverse powers of evil, a theme as relevant to today's world as it was to the world of yesterday.

———

Every once in a while a good unknown writer gets anointed, the Pulitzer committee issues a prize, and sales jump. Still, for every winner there are scores of writers who are as good but are virtually unread. To that list of unknown writers, good writers toiling in obscurity, add the name of Alexander Blackburn.

— *The Dallas Morning News*

Colorado Noir is a walk on the dark and wild side of America's most controversial city. Ten stories and one novella.

$16.95 at bookstores everywhere, or direct from the publisher:
www.rhyolitepress.com

ISBN 978-0-9896763-0-4

"This guy is the next Tom Clancy"
Bill Hill, USAF (Ret)

Colorado Noir by John Dwaine McKenna
is our first multiple award-winning publication

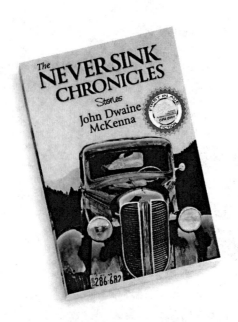

<u>Praise for *The Neversink Chronicles*</u>

"A gifted and natural born story teller with command of dialog and dialect. Congratulations!"
—Clark Secrest, Author, *Hells Bells,* San Diego, CA

"A gifted storyteller. An amazing first book. Keep writing, you have a great future ahead of you."
—Allison Auch, Copy Editor, Durango, CO

"Hated parting with the manuscript, as I knew things were changing quickly in *Neversink.* That's when you know you have a great book in your hands."
—*Leigh Daily*, Paralegal, Boulder, CO

"This is a book to read over and over. The people are real, the life is true and the author has to have been everywhere and met everyone to have captured all of these personalities so well. I'm waiting for more from him."
—Mary Lelia, Austin,Texas

" 'Just Another Day', gave me chills remembering my own Vietnam experience".
—Skip Mooney, Financial Consultant, Manitou Springs, CO

". . . and the winner, First Prize for fiction, 2012 goes to . . .
The Neversink Chronicles"
18th Annual CIPA Awards Ceremony
Denver, CO May 17, 2012

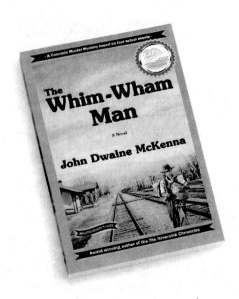

The Whim - Wham Man

A STORY THAT HAS IT ALL . . .
A CRIME YOU CAN'T FORGIVE
A PLOT YOU COULDN'T IMAGINE
AND A CHARACTER . . .
YOU'LL NEVER FORGET!

There's no sanitary way to write about murder. "The Whim-Wham Man," a gut-punching novel of a teen-aged boy whose idyllic life in rural Colorado comes crashing down when reality and adulthood rush in after the brutalization and savage killing of two young girls . . . **It's a helluva yarn.**

CIPA EVVY Award Winner, 2013
2nd prize, Best Fiction

$15 at bookstores everywhere, or direct from the publisher:
www.rhyolitepress.com

ISBN 978-0-9839952-2-7

Praise for *The Boy Who Slept with Bears*

I loved this book and didn't want it to end as I grew to understand Tomas and his relationship with the earth and brother bear. A great book for young and old alike.

—Valorie R. Hornsby

George Douthit's book *The Boy Who Slept with Bears*, is the moving story of a Southern Ute boy coming of age at a time when the Ute traditional territories were being overrun by non indians during the gold rush and the Utes removed to reservations. The author captures the boy's desire to avenge his father's murder at the hands of white soldiers. He steps from boyhood into a man's world while struggling to hold onto his traditional beliefs. Though fictional, Douthit weaves true historical details of the Southern Utes and a legendary grizzly bear named "Old Mose" into a masterful story that leaves the reader enthralled and captivated.

—Vickie Leigh Krudwig, Author, *Searching for Chipeta*

A terrific read for both young and old! Outstanding! *The Boy Who Slept with Bear* is the best book about native Americans I've ever read. Please send two more copies for my nephews.

—Leonard Foxworth

Prune Pie
And Other Moving Stories
by Victoria Ward

The heartfelt stories in *Prune Pie* are laced with humor and truth and spoken in clear, homespun language that is both compelling and entertaining. Don't miss Victoria Ward's true tales of her life on the road with the soulmate and cowboy troubadour husband she calls "Bear".

$15 at bookstores everywhere, or direct from the publisher:
www.rhyolitepress.com

ISBN 978-1-943829-00-2
eBook ISBN 978-1-943829-01-9

"Life on the road can be rather mundane for a cowboy singer. That is, unless your wife is traveling with you, and can find humor in every situation. In *Prune Pie & Other Moving Stories*, Victoria Ward not only pokes fun at her award-winning husband, Barry Ward, but she also occasionally owns up to her own blunders. You don't even have to like cowboy music to enjoy these stories. This is a fun read."

— Orin Friesen   KFDI Radio, Wichita, Kansas

CPSIA information can be obtained
at www.ICGtesting.com
Printed in the USA
FSOW02n0907141017
39913FS